Wyoming

OFF THE BEATEN PATH™

OFF THE BEATEN PATH SERIES

Wyoming

OFF THE BEATEN PATH™

FIRST EDITION

MARY BUCKINGHAM MATURI
RICHARD J. MATURI

A Voyager Book

The Globe Pequot Press

Old Saybrook, Connecticut

Illustrations by Carole Drong
Cover map copyright © DeLorme Mapping

Off the Beaten Path is a trademark of The Globe Pequot Press, Inc.
The brands depicted on page xvi are reprinted from *Official List Wyoming Brands 1900.*

Library of Congress Cataloging-in-Publication Data
Maturi, Mary Buckingham.
    Wyoming: off the beaten path / Mary Buckingham Maturi,
Richard J. Maturi.
        p.   cm. — (Off the beaten path series)
        "A Voyager book."
        Includes index.
        ISBN 1-56440-854-X
        1. Wyoming—Guidebooks.   I. Maturi, Richard J.   II. Title.   III. Series.
F759.3.M37   1996
917.8704'33—dc20
                                                                96-11671
                                                                CIP

Manufactured in the United States of America
First Edition/First Printing

To Wyoming, "the way the West was . . ."

Wyoming

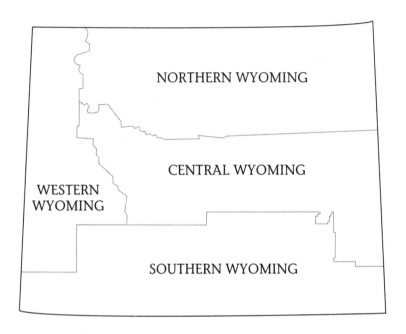

NORTHERN WYOMING

CENTRAL WYOMING

WESTERN WYOMING

SOUTHERN WYOMING

CONTENTS

Introduction

For many generations Wyoming was a place one traveled through to other destinations. Likewise my wife, Mary, and I journeyed through Wyoming numerous times before we decided to move to "The Cowboy State." Back in 1971 we stopped at the Lincoln monument between Cheyenne and Laramie. Enthralled by the beauty of the area, I looked at Mary and said, "Wouldn't it be great to live out here?"

Well, Rick is always one for planning ahead, and almost twenty years later we moved to a log home in the Laramie Range of the Wyoming Rockies less than 15 miles from that very spot. I agree with him that we found a great place to live.

During the past five years, we discovered many of Wyoming's hidden treasures, from interesting people to unique and historical places, while on assignment for local and regional publications. We ferreted out the Jackalope Capital of the World, Wyoming's own Don Quixote (a seventy-year-old retired engineer who resurrected the world's largest wind turbine), and out-of-the-way communities such as Meeteetse, with 368 residents, a nearly one-hundred-year-old mercantile store, and three fine museums. In the following pages of *Wyoming: Off the Beaten Path* we invite you to join our journey to the "Way the West Was."

Today, more than ever, Americans and foreigners seeking fascinating and unusual places to visit make Wyoming their main destination. Wyoming abounds with historical significance, breathtaking scenery, and secluded places in which to forget the pressures of daily life and recapture your soul.

Within Wyoming's 97,194 square miles (it's the ninth largest state) lies a wide variety of terrain, from the high plains to the river valleys and from the badlands to the mountains. Wyoming's altitude ranges from the Belle Fourche River at 3,100 feet to Gannett Peak at 13,804 feet. Numerous pioneer trails left their mark on the Wyoming landscape, just as the roughness of the country left its mark on the character of the people who made Wyoming their home.

Today's traveler can still capture a sense of the rugged individualism and community and pioneer spirit that built this great land of ours by following the Bozeman, California, Emigrant, Jim Bridger, Mormon, Oregon, Overland, Nez Perce, Texas Cattle, and Pony Express trails, which traversed the Wyoming countryside. Through the centuries, the numerous tracks across Wyoming started with the dinosaurs and moved through time with the ancient peoples, Native Americans, rendezvous men, soldiers stationed at military outposts, and the pioneers. As transportation evolved, Wyoming was crisscrossed by the railroad, the pony express, stagecoach routes, the Lincoln Highway (the nation's first transcontinental highway), and today's interstate highway system.

The state is a geologist's paradise and its terrain is often described as the work of a madman. The State of Wyoming welcome signs at the borders proclaim, LIKE NO PLACE ON EARTH. Although technically speaking the signs should read, LIKE NO OTHER PLACE ON EARTH, the misstatement seems accurate when you gaze out over Hell's Half Acre and other equally stunning Wyoming geological sites. Often, the seemingly barren landscape is interrupted by incredibly beautiful outcroppings of wildflowers.

The state's terrain covers many geologic periods, and the upheavals through the ages have left geologic time exposed as one rarely sees in other areas of the world. The high mountain ranges date back to the Precambrian Age and are more than 3 billion years old. Numerous mountain ranges, state and national forests, and state and national parks present ample opportunity to get off the beaten path and explore the wilderness.

Wyoming boasts the largest concentration of large and small mammals in the lower forty-eight states. Across the wide, open spaces you can discover antelope (pronghorns), bears, bighorn sheep, buffalo, coyotes, cranes, eagles, elk, falcons, ferrets, geese, hawks, loons, moose, mountain goats, mountain lions, mule and white-tailed deer, prairie dogs, swans, turkey vultures, and, if you look close enough, jackalopes (a fictional cross between a jackrabbit and an antelope).

There are some caveats to be aware of when you venture into Wyoming. Roadside rest areas on the main thoroughfares sometimes are few and far between and virtually nonexistent on the less-traveled roads. Take a cue from the Boy Scouts, and "Be Prepared." The weather can change quickly and drastically in the span of a few hours or miles. Dress appropriately and carry extra gear, water, and food in the event of car trouble, inclement weather, or some other emergency. On some roads you won't see another soul for hours. In most Wyoming locations you are thousands of feet closer to the sun than in many other states. Use sunblock to protect your skin from burn and wear a hat to cut down on the glare of the sun's rays. Prevent altitude sickness by drinking plenty of water to keep your fluids at the proper level. And if you plan to do some horseback riding, here's a tip from a woman who recently returned from a long cattle drive: "Be sure to wear spandex or similar bicycle pants under your jeans to prevent saddle sores and chafing."

That's all there is to it, pardner. Pull on your cowboy boots, cinch down your cowboy hat, and enjoy the ride. Welcome to Wyoming.

Mary Buckingham Maturi
Richard J. Maturi
Cheramie, Wyoming

The prices and rates listed in this guidebook were confirmed at press time. We recommend, however, that you call establishments before traveling to obtain current information. Meal price ranges used in this book are as follows: inexpensive (less than $6), moderate (between $6 and $12), and expensive (more than $12). The area code for all of Wyoming is 307.

Acknowledgments

Special thanks to the Wyoming Division of Tourism, Bureau of Land Management, National Park Service, United States Forest Service, Wyoming State Parks & Historic Sites, and local chambers of commerce for providing information and materials to help begin our quest for the real West in *Wyoming: Off the Beaten Path*. Finally, thanks to the interesting people of Wyoming for making our project such an enjoyable journey.

Wyoming

OFF THE BEATEN PATH™

Wyoming brands

SOUTHERN WYOMING

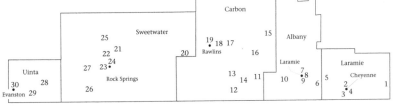

Carbon

Sweetwater

25

22 · 21
· 24
23

20

19
· 18 17
Rawlins

15

Albany

16

Laramie

7
· 8
9

Laramie

Cheyenne

27

Uinta

28

Rock Springs

26

13
14 11

12

10

5

6

2
· 4
3

1

30
·
Evanston 29

1. High Plains Archaeology Labs
2. Cheyenne Frontier Days Old West Museum
3. Terry Bison Ranch
4. Rainsford Inn Bed and Breakfast
5. A. Drummond's Ranch Bed and Breakfast
6. Vedauwoo
7. Wyoming Territorial Park
8. Geological Museum
9. The Overland Restaurant
10. Vee Bar Guest Ranch
11. Lake Marie
12. Grand Encampment Museum
13. Hotel Wolf
14. Brush Creek Ranch
15. Virginian Hotel
16. Elk Mountain Trading Company
17. Fort Fred Steele
18. Parco Inn
19. Wyoming Frontier Prison
20. Henry B. Joy Monument
21. 1921 Union Hall
22. Reliance Tipple
23. Natural History Museum
24. Sha Hol Dee B&B
25. Killpecker Dune Field
26. Flaming Gorge National Recreation Area
27. Sweetwater County Historical Museum
28. Fort Bridger State Historic Site
29. Piedmont Kilns
30. Joss House

SOUTHERN WYOMING

LARAMIE COUNTY

Entering southeast Wyoming from the east, you cross ancient Native American trails and the Texas Cattle Trail. Forsake Interstate 80 and cross the border from Nebraska on Highway 30, the old Lincoln Highway (located just north of Interstate 80). An abandoned wooden service station greets you with NEB/WYO painted in the middle of the dilapidated structure to indicate the state border.

The idea for the Lincoln Highway originated at a 1912 dinner meeting of automobile industry tycoons in Indianapolis. At the time, the nation's two million miles of roads were largely unconnected. Railroads represented the only practical means of coast-to-coast travel. Within three years a patchwork made from existing roads wound its way across the country from Times Square in New York City to Lincoln Park in San Francisco, creating the first transcontinental highway. Wyoming lit bonfires along the route across the state on November 13, 1913, to signal the opening of the new Lincoln Highway.

Later improvements made the Lincoln Highway one of the premier roads of its day. The federal government took over the road system in the late 1920s. To mark the event the Boy Scouts of America installed more than three thousand Lincoln Highway markers along every mile of the route on September 1, 1928.

For the most part, the Lincoln Highway ran parallel to the Union Pacific Railroad, which preceded the highway west. Today, fiber-optic cables transport modern-day telecommunications along this historic travel corridor.

The area around the border town of Pine Bluffs served as a frontier crossroads for prehistoric peoples, pioneers, and cattle drives. The nearby pine hills provided the Native American inhabitants excellent campsites with plentiful water, firewood, and small game. The **Texas Trail Museum** (housed in the town's original 1915 power plant) at Third and Market Streets features the importance of Pine Bluffs Crossroads in the development of the area and the West. You will also find historic displays on the area's cattle ranches and homesteads, antique fire equipment, Native American culture and the Lincoln Highway. The museum is located in the **Texas Trail Park,** where you can

2

explore a caboose, railroad boardinghouse, blacksmith shop, homesteader's log cabin, and bunkhouse. The Pine Bluffs rail station served as an important cattle-shipping center for many years. More than six hundred thousand cattle were driven through the Pine Bluffs Crossroads area during the heyday of the Texas Cattle Trail in 1871. The Texas Trail Park and Texas Trail Museum are open 9:00 A.M. to 5:00 P.M. from the first week in May to the last week in September or by appointment. Call 245–3713 for information.

The ◆ **High Plains Archaeology Labs** at 217 West Third Street and the nearby excavation sites are open to visitors during summer months. The archaeological dig is being conducted by the University of Wyoming. Crews of students under the direction of Charles Rehrer have uncovered nomadic Native American artifacts dating back nearly ten thousand years. Artifacts from the dig are on display at the archaeology labs. The dig site is a short walk away and is situated west of the Pine Bluffs rest area south of Interstate 80, where you will also find a tourist information center and a grouping of painted tipis and ancient tipi rings. Check at the archaeology labs for directions and dig site access. For information call the Pine Bluffs Chamber of Commerce at 245–3695.

The painted tipis are painstakingly researched re-creations of the symbols and colors employed by the Sioux Nation. Native American paints were created from animals, minerals, and plants and applied to a damp hide. After the hide dried, the coloring became permanent and was protected with a "varnish" made out of the juice of the prickly pear cactus. While many symbols were shared by the various tribes, the interpretations of some colors and symbols differed from tribe to tribe.

Tipis were made out of buffalo hides sewn together by the women with sinew from buffalo tendons. The hard, dry end of the sinew formed the needle, and the women kept the rest of the sinew pliable for sewing by keeping it moist in the mouth.

Tipi designs were inspired by a number of sources, such as the owner's dreams, powers, experiences, visions, and battle victories. Common Sioux symbols included hoops representing the sacred circle that signified unity of the people, the world, and completeness of life. Four colored stripes represented the four sacred directions: red for east and a new day, new beginnings, and hope; black for west and life-giving rains, rest, and loving; white for north and the giant cold winds of winter, strength, and endurance; and yellow for south and warm winds, growth, and understanding.

Take time to enjoy a trail walk around the archaeological dig and rest area with the aid of a guidebook (available at the visitor center) and interpretive trail signs pointing out wildlife habitat areas, bird sites and native grasses and other vegetation found in the **Pine Bluffs Nature Area.**

If you are in the area during the first week of August, check out the **Pine Bluffs Trail Days Celebration,** complete with wagon train, cowboy poet, melodrama, parade, rodeo, street dance, and Western Bar-B-Ques. For information call 778–7200.

Forty-five miles west through the high plains alongside Interstate 80, you will arrive at the capital city of Cheyenne and catch your first glimpse of the majestic Rocky Mountains climbing up out of the plains. Cheyenne derives its name from Shey'an'nah, an Algonquin Indian tribe. Cheyenne's wild and woolly past started with the arrival of the Union Pacific Railroad and establishment of Fort D. A. Russell (now F. E. Warren Air Force Base) for protection of the railroaders in 1867. Major General Grenville M. Dodge, a Union Pacific surveyor, plotted the city as a major rail terminus before the long climb over the Laramie Range.

Early residents besides the railroaders included mule skinners, soldiers, rustlers, stagecoach hands, outlaws, and other opportunists. The railhead made Cheyenne a natural headquarters for numerous cattle barons, who established the elaborate Cheyenne Club where they conducted cattle business and hosted lavish parties. A marker for the Cheyenne Club stands at the corner of Warren Avenue and Seventeenth Street.

In the late 1800s Cheyenne also became an important center for outfitting miners headed toward the goldfields in the Black Hills, and a stagecoach line ran between the two areas. The Cheyenne–Fort Laramie–Deadwood Trail started from the corner of Capital Avenue and Sixteenth Street and ended in Deadwood, South Dakota. A trail marker is located at the corner of Capital Avenue and Twenty-second Street.

There's plenty to see and do around Cheyenne. The city is home to the "Daddy of 'em All," **Cheyenne Frontier Days.** While the majority of visitors flock to the world's oldest and largest outdoor rodeo, take a diversion to the expanded and refurbished ❖ **Cheyenne Frontier Days Old West Museum** located in Frontier Park at 4501 North Carey Avenue.

This truly fine museum is a "must stop" if you want to capture the real flavor of the West. An extensive collection of horse-drawn vehicles includes stagecoaches, a hearse, and a range chuck wagon. Native American clothing, rodeo memorabilia dating back to the first rodeo in 1897 (Cheyenne Frontier Days will celebrate its hundredth year in 1996), a rustic saloon, a Union Pacific exhibit, exhibits on Cheyenne history, and a wonderful collection of Western art comprise the rest of the displays. You'll learn about Will Pickett, the African-American cowboy who invented bulldogging by throwing a steer using only his teeth. The museum is open year-round, seven days a week. Call 778–7290 for summer and winter hours.

Another worthwhile experience of Cheyenne Frontier Days is **The Indian Village** located near the entrance to Frontier Park at Eighth Street and Carey Avenue. Award-winning Native American dancers from tribes across the nation convene here and give free dance performances several times daily during Frontier Days. Authentic Native American jewelry, clothing, and other items are available for sale to the public. Frontier Days runs from the last full week of July for ten days. For information call (800) 227–6336.

Nearby, the **Cheyenne Botanic Gardens** offer a pleasant diversion from the dusty grounds of Frontier Park. Sit outside among the flowers, take a stroll along the garden pathways, or investigate the exotic plants in the greenhouse section. See, smell, and touch the inviting oasis. It is the only botanic garden in the nation that offers social services, education, and therapy to seniors, youths at risk, and handicapped individuals. The gardens are located at 710 South Lions Park Drive. Hours are Monday through Friday from 8:30 A.M. to 4:30 P.M. and Saturday, Sunday, and holidays from 11:00 A.M. to 3:30 P.M. Admission is free but donations are welcome. The phone number is 637–6458.

For a sparsely populated state, Wyoming showcases a fine **State Capitol** that is worthy of a tour. Its twenty-four-carat gold-leaf dome commands the skyline from all entrances to the city. Built from 1886 to 1890, the Capitol features Corinthian columns and sandstone quarried at Rawlins and in Colorado. A statue commemorating Esther Hobart Morris, the first woman justice of the peace and a prominent force in the women's suffrage movement, graces the entrance to the Capitol. A replica of this statue is also located in Statuary Hall in the U.S. Capitol in Washington, D.C.

Wyoming has been designated as the Equality State. Its first Territorial Legislature granted women the right to vote in 1869, and later the legislature required that women be allowed to vote in Wyoming as a condition of Wyoming's entrance into the Union in 1890. The Nineteenth Amendment giving all women citizens of the United States the right to vote was not passed until 1919. Wyoming also swore in the first all-female jury and elected the first female governor, Nellie Tayloe Ross, in a 1924 special election to replace her husband, Governor William B. Ross, who had died in office. In 1933 Franklin D. Roosevelt appointed Nellie Tayloe Ross director of the U.S. Mint, a post she held until her retirement in 1953.

The Spirit of Wyoming, a bronze statue on the plaza between the Capitol and the Herschler Building, stands over 18 feet in height and depicts a cowboy and his horse at odds against nature and its elements. The statue is the work of international award-winning sculptor Edward J. Fraughton.

Inside, pay particular attention to the eight large murals in the Senate and House of Representatives chambers. They illustrate early Wyoming life and are titled *Chief Cheyenne, Frontier Cavalry Officers, Pony Express Rider, Railroad/Builders/Surveyors, Cattlemen, Trappers, Homesteaders,* and *Stagecoach.* The ceilings of both chambers are inlaid with striking Tiffany stained glass crafted with the Wyoming State Seal as the focal point. Proceed to room 302 where a 1982 mural, *Wyoming, the Land, the People,* by Mike Kopriva shows Wyoming's past and present culture and lifestyles. Before you exit the Capitol, take a look at the mounted elk (wapiti) and bison to get an up-close perspective of the size of Wyoming wildlife. The Capitol is open to the public Monday through Friday from 8:00 A.M. to 5:00 P.M. and on Saturday from the first Saturday in May to the last Saturday in August from 9:00 A.M. to 5:00 P.M. Tours are available year-round. For information on access and in-session activities call 777–7220. The Capitol is located on Capitol Avenue and Twenty-second Street.

Now that you have seen where the legislature works, take a short walk over to the 1904 **Historic Governors' Mansion** on 300 East Twenty-first Street. The Mansion housed nineteen Wyoming First Families until replaced by a modern residence in

1976. Designed by Omaha architect Charles Mudrock, the building features Colonial Revival architecture with a portico supported by four Corinthian columns flanking the main entrance. A tour video is available for viewing. The Historic Governors' Mansion is open year-round Tuesday through Saturday from 9:00 A.M. to 5:00 P.M. but is closed at the noon hour during the winter months. Call 777–7878 for more information.

The **Wyoming State Museum,** which celebrated its centennial in 1995, houses major collections covering territorial days, Wyoming's first families, Native Americans, Western art, Hollywood Westerns with movie star Tim McCoy (once an adjutant general of the Wyoming National Guard), and Wyoming fossils and petroglyphs (rock carvings). One of the museum's treasures is the Historic Photographic Collection comprising some 250,000 images from such famed photographers as Joseph E. Stimson and W. H. Jackson, dating back to the 1860s. Photo subjects range from cattle brands to robberies and from the Teapot Dome to Yellowstone National Park. The Wyoming State Museum is open Monday through Friday from 8:30 A.M. to 5:00 P.M. Saturday and Sunday hours vary from summer to winter. For more information call 777–7022.

A trip to Cheyenne would not be complete without a trip to **Lakeview Cemetery,** in operation for more than 115 years. Among the more interesting and unusual deaths recorded in cemetery records are an 1887 death attributed to drinking ice water, an 1892 execution of a seventeen-year-old, and a 1902 death from flypaper poisoning. Many early deaths in the area were caused by railroad-related accidents, shootings, and flu epidemics. The first hanging by a mob occurred in 1883, the first streetcar death in 1903, the first automobile death in 1915, and the first airplane death in 1923. Wander among the tombstones to search out your own historical gems. Lakeview Cemetery is an operational cemetery, so act accordingly and do not interfere with funeral services. It is located at 2501 Seymour Avenue. The cemetery gates are always open but the office is only open Monday through Friday 8:00 A.M. to 5:00 P.M.

If you are interested in unique architecture, take a walk on the **Historic Downtown Walking Tour** featured on the city map available at the visitor's bureau at 309 West Sixteenth Street. For information call 778–3133. Three of our favorites are the 1886

Union Pacific Depot (currently being renovated to house the Transportation Museum), the Tivoli Building, and the Dineen automobile dealership with some imposing lions near the roof. Cheyenne also has several wonderful art galleries and Western clothing stores, which you'll pass on the walking tour.

By now the digestive juices should be flowing. For a fresh sandwich, espresso, and tempting desserts, we suggest **Matilda's** at 1651 Carey Avenue, number 11 in the mall downtown. Check out the soups and daily specials. If you are lucky, they will have their green chili and cheese corn muffins. They also serve breakfast, with pastries baked daily in the tiny kitchen. Matilda's is open Monday through Friday from 7:30 A.M. to 4:30 P.M. and Saturday 9:00 A.M. to 3:00 P.M. Food prices are inexpensive. For information call 635–4896.

For more substantial evening fare, you can't beat the **Cheyenne Cattle Company** for steaks, seafood, and other favorites. The Cheyenne Cattle Company is located at 1700 West Lincolnway. It opens for evening meals at 5:30 P.M. Food prices are moderate to expensive. Call 638–3301.

The ◆ **Terry Bison Ranch** was formerly the southern headquarters of the huge land holdings of Wyoming's first governor, F. E. Warren. Presidents, generals, and senators found it a pleasant retreat. Visitors to Warren's Terry Ranch included President Theodore Roosevelt and General John "Blackjack" Pershing. Today, you can bunk in a log cabin or park your RV and enjoy summer Hells on Wheels rodeo action, chuck-wagon dinners, horseback riding, fishing on a private lake, and motorized tours to a bison herd of two thousand roaming thirty thousand acres— all within minutes of downtown Cheyenne. The Terry Bison Trailblazers sing cowboy songs such as "Cool Water" as you dig into your fixin's. Other facilities on the Terry Bison Ranch include the Senator's Steakhouse and Brass Buffalo Saloon and Terry Ranch Cellars, Wyoming's first winery. Take the Terry Ranch exit off Interstate 25, 7 miles south of Cheyenne, and follow the signs. The season runs from Memorial Day to Labor Day but the cabins and RV facilities are available year-round. The rodeo entrance fee is $5.00 for adults, $4.00 for seniors, and $1.00 for children under twelve, and cabins rent in the $50 to $80 range depending on the season. Food prices are moderate. For more information call 634–4171.

For early birds, guided tours of **F. E. Warren Air Force Base** are conducted by appointment. For information call 775–3381. Take Randall Avenue to the F. E. Warren Air Force Base (formerly Fort D. A. Russell) main entrance on the west end of Cheyenne. The tour includes an excellent museum depicting the fort's early military history. Many of the older buildings, some dating back to 1885, are constructed in Colonial style of red brick with large white columns. A new Archaeology Interpretive Center showcases Native American artifacts uncovered by the base's excavation program.

Originally a cavalry outpost, the base now operates some two hundred of the Strategic Air Command's Minute Man III intercontinental ballistic missiles over a three-state area. In 1930 President Hoover renamed the fort in honor of Francis Emory Warren, Wyoming's first governor and a U.S. senator for thirty-seven years. Warren came to Wyoming in 1868 at age twenty-three, taking a job with A. R. Converse, owner of a mercantile store. The two became partners in the mercantile business and later in livestock operations. The Warren Mercantile Company grew into the largest supplier of furniture and hardware in Wyoming, and Warren's livestock holdings grew to three thousand cattle and more than sixty thousand sheep. By 1909 Warren ranked as the richest person in Wyoming. The rest is history.

During Frontier Days, the air force base hosts Fort D. A. Russell Days with a milk-can dinner (a meal usually consisting of sausage, potatoes, and corn, originally cooked in a milk can) followed by a dance where you can do the Virginia reel under lantern light. Tickets are a modest $11 for a night of great fun. Guests are asked to come attired in Victorian period costume or Western wear. Other activities include artillery demonstrations and infantry and cavalry horse drills of the 1800s.

For a delightful night's rest, step back in time and check in to the historically renovated ◆ **Rainsford Inn Bed and Breakfast,** listed on the National Register of Historic Places as part of the Rainsford Historic District. George D. Rainsford was a rancher who came to Wyoming in the late 1870s. One of the building's former owners was Willis Van De Vanter, the only Wyoming judge to sit on the U.S. Supreme Court. Your host, Nancy Drege, purchased the property in 1991 and received a Certified Historic Restoration Award in 1992.

Many antiques, heirlooms, and works of local artists await your browsing. You have your choice of five spacious suites, one of which is handicapped accessible. The School Room reflects Nancy's earlier career while the Cattle Baron Room has a Western flavor. For those romantic occasions, the Moonlight and Roses Room is just the right touch. Four of the suites have whirlpool tubs.

In the morning you have your choice of several delectable breakfasts. Rooms are between $61 and $95 with a 10 percent discount for seniors, military personnel, AAA members, and business guests. The Rainsford Inn is located at 219 East Eighteenth Street. For reservations call 638–BEDS.

From Cheyenne take Missile Drive to **Happy Jack Road** (Highway 210) headed west. This scenic back way to Laramie rises from Cheyenne's elevation of 6,062 feet to over 8,640 feet before you descend into Laramie. The terrain changes dramatically as the rolling grasslands give way to the craggy outcroppings of the foothills of the Laramie Range. Piney aromas overtake the smell of grass and sage. Keep alert for antelope, coyotes, deer, elk, and other wildlife.

Happy Jack Road derives its name from Happy Jack Hollinsworth, who started ranching in the foothills of the Laramie Range in 1884. Jack was always singing and whistling while working his ranch and hauling wood for sale in Cheyenne.

Twenty-six miles out of Cheyenne you will come upon the entrance to 1,645 acre **Curt Gowdy State Park,** an excellent spot to camp, hike, and fish. The park encompasses Crystal and Granite reservoirs, the water supply for Cheyenne. There's a minimal $2.00 entrance fee per vehicle ($3.00 for out-of-state vehicles), or you can camp for $4.00 per night. The park is named after native son and world-renowned sportscaster Curt Gowdy. Towering rock formations provide a beautiful backdrop for a relaxing day. Long before whites arrived, the area was a favorite campground for Native Americans including the Comanche, Crow, Shoshone, Cheyenne, Arapahoe, and Sioux.

Across Happy Jack Road to the north and less than a mile west is Hynds Lodge, built by Cheyenne businessman and philanthropist Harry P. Hynds and donated to the Boy Scouts of America. The building is open to large and small groups from June 1 through October 1 on a reservation-only basis. The reservations office is open starting from the first working day of January, from

10

8:30 A.M. to 3:30 P.M. The lodge includes sleeping accommodations for thirty; a large kitchen complete with appliances, pots and pans, and dishes; a dining area; and recreational facilities. Within walking distance, an amphitheater set amid a backdrop of gigantic boulders and rock formations hosts the **Happy Jack Mountain Music Festival** in June each year. For information on Hynds Lodge and the festival, call Curt Gowdy State Park headquarters at 632–7946.

You may want to stay and explore this beautiful area for a day or two. For an ideal experience try ◆ **A. Drummond's Ranch Bed and Breakfast.** Your host, Taydie, makes memories. Meals become an artistic celebration with fresh herbs garnishing delicious homemade food served on china with fresh linen and pearl-handled silverware. The living room invites you to gaze at breathtaking mountain scenery and the many perennial flowers. When you are in the mood for grazing, plentiful snacks are at your fingertips.

Terry-cloth robes await your use, as do Jacuzzi tubs adjacent to two of the four guest rooms. The Carriage House loft will be your ultimate getaway with grand views, a gas fireplace, a private dining area complete with a miniature chandelier, and a deck with a gas cooking grill and your private Jacuzzi.

You set your own pace and choose your favorite activity such as hiking, horseback riding, mountain biking, cross-country skiing, or quiet relaxation. The variety of resident animals, from goats to geese and from llamas to horses, will bring out the kid in almost everyone.

Rates range from $60 to $175 per night and include breakfast. Personalized tour packages are also available, as is boarding for horses. For reservations call 634–6042. Drummond's is located at 399 Happy Jack Road, several miles east of the entrance to Curt Gowdy State Park.

ALBANY COUNTY

Continuing west on Happy Jack Road you are greeted by Albany County's fantastic natural rock formations in the ◆ **Vedauwoo** (pronounced *Vee*-dah-voo) area. The name means "earthborn spirits" in Arapahoe, and Native Americans regarded the area as a sacred place. With a little bit of imagination you can have a great

11

Vedauwoo

deal of fun deciphering the shapes into familiar objects sculpted by eons of wind and weather. Our favorite is the one we call Seal Rock, just north of the highway and a few hundred yards before you reach the large Medicine Bow National Forest sign as you approach from the east. A few hundred yards beyond the forest sign, turn left (south) to seek out other interesting rock formations and reach the Vedauwoo picnic area. Happy Jack Road continues on to the Lincoln Monument, where you will arrive after a bit more sightseeing.

You'll have to discover Bison, Loaf of Bread, Hawk, and Dinosaur Bone rocks on your own. Be sure to look west for the precariously balanced cube as you head south on the winding dirt road. Take your time, or the washboard road will bounce you out of your seat. Your vista provides good views of Twin Mountain, Green Mountain to the east, and Pole Mountain to the west. Vedauwoo offers a refuge in which to contemplate your own spirit, and the more active and adventuresome can scale Potato Chip Rock, located near the picnic area, with difficulty ratings from 5.00 to 5.14. Time your visit to Vedauwoo so that you can join in on a **Moonlight Interpretive Walk** on the nights of the full moon. Each month focuses on a special theme, such as the Spirit Moon at Vedauwoo or the Pika Moon in the alpine mountains. To confirm moonlight walk dates, times, and meeting places, call the Medicine Bow National Forest office at 745–8971 or stop in at the Forest Service headquarters at 2468 Jackson Street in Laramie.

After this respite, continue on the Vedauwoo road until you encounter Interstate 80, but before joining the rush of traffic take a brief detour to **Ames Monument.** Proceed through the underpass and bear to the left and a 2-mile trip will take you to a 60-foot pyramid of native granite built in 1882 for $65,000 as a monument to Oliver and Oakes Ames, who helped finance the construction of the first transcontinental railroad.

Designed by noted architect Henry Hobson Richardson, the pyramid appears to be smack in the middle of nowhere. The monument exhibits the heavy stonework characteristic of the Romanesque-influenced architectural style made famous by Richardson. Originally the monument stood next to the Union Pacific tracks and the now-abandoned town site of Sherman, where the trains were safety inspected before they attempted the steep descent into Laramie from Sherman Hill. Around the turn of the century, the railroad moved the tracks a few miles to the south in order to use a more desirable grade. As a result, Sherman died a ghost town's death. U.S. senator Oakes Ames did not fare much better. He was indicted for bribery in connection with the famous Credit Mobilier Scandal but died before he could be brought to justice.

While the Ames brothers helped unite the country by rail, the next monument on the tour commemorates the man who kept the nation united and gave his name to the country's first transcontinental highway: Abraham Lincoln. Complete the loop back to Interstate 80 and proceed to the summit of Sherman Hill, the highest spot on the coast-to-coast highway, with an elevation of 8,640 feet. Built in 1959, the **Lincoln Monument** originally stood alongside the Lincoln Highway route but was moved in 1969 to its present site. University of Wyoming art professor and sculptor Robert Russin crafted the 12½-foot bronze bust, which rises 42½ feet on a granite pedestal built with stone from the Vedauwoo area. There are a visitors center, rest area, and picnic sites at the summit. Happy Jack Road also completes its journey here, joining Interstate 80 at the summit. Backtracking about a mile on Happy Jack Road takes you to **Tie City** where tie hackers once fashioned railroad ties out of logs. Today it is a trailhead for cross-country skiers in the winter and hikers the rest of the year.

Get ready for a spectacular descent into the Laramie Basin through a canyon lined on both sides by red rock. Ancient tipi rings, buffalo kill sites, and unearthed artifacts indicate that nomadic peoples frequented this area for at least ten thousand years, but it was not until the Union Pacific Railroad arrived in 1868 that a permanent settlement took hold. Named after Jacques LaRamie, a French Canadian fur trapper and the first white man thought to have visited the area (LaRamie shipped furs out from 1815 to 1827), the city was selected by the Wyoming Territorial Legislature as the site of the Wyoming Territorial Prison and the University of Wyoming.

The Overland Trail traversed the Laramie Basin, which was served by a large station complete with a blacksmith shop, road-house, and toll bridge to cross the Laramie River at the Big Laramie Station. Westbound travelers used the trail heavily between 1862 and 1868, before the Union Pacific Railroad made the journey more convenient and less treacherous. Overland Trail ruts can still be seen stretching out across the prairie along Highway 130 approximately 11 miles west of Laramie.

An "end of the tracks" town, Laramie gained a reputation as a rough place. In October 1868 a fierce gun battle broke out between outlaws and vigilantes. The criminals fled, but not before four were caught and hanged. Asa Moore, Con Wager, "Big Ed," and "Big Steve" had been accused of fifty murders combined.

The first all-woman jury sat in Laramie in 1870. King William of Prussia sent President Grant a congratulatory message. The breakthrough proved short-lived, however, since women did not serve on juries again until 1950. On another suffrage front, Laramie's Grandma Louiza Swain went to the polls in 1871 and earned the distinction of being the first woman in the world to vote in a general election.

Restored to its original 1890s condition, the Wyoming Territorial Prison lives on as a State Historical Site under the name of **❖ Wyoming Territorial Park.** Although only in operation for a few years, the park has earned the reputation as a class act. The prison was the only one to incarcerate the leader of the "Wild Bunch," Butch Cassidy (Robert Leroy Parker), for horse thievery. He did not serve out his two-year term. Governor William A. Richards pardoned him in January 1896, but not until Butch gave his oath as a gentleman that he would do no more thievin' of horses or cattle or banks in Wyoming. Butch kept his word, but train robberies were not part of the bargain. Here you will also learn about infamous prisoners such as Clark "The Kid" Pelton, Minnie Snyder, and evildoers of all kinds. Another colorful character, Calamity Jane, comes to life in the person of one of her kin. Norma Rose Slack portrays her great-great-aunt in convincing fashion.

There's a re-created Wyoming Frontier Town on-site so you can grab a sarsaparilla while you watch the Belle of the West Saloon girls sing, or you can sit back and take a stagecoach ride. The park is also home to the National U.S. Marshalls Museum, covering more than two hundred years of law-enforcement history.

The performers at the Horse Barn Dinner Theater entertain you with a top-quality, rip-roaring show while you are served a filling meal, all for $25 or under. Special events occur all season long, including the Laramie River Black Powder Shoot & Mountainman Rendezvous and U.S. Marshalls' Day, which attracts mounted marshalls from across the country. For park and dinner theater information call (800) 845–2287. The Wyoming Territorial Park is located in the west end of Laramie at 975 Snowy Range Road.

Besides having a beautiful tree-lined campus, the University of Wyoming (founded in 1886, four years before Wyoming became a state) has some unique treasures hidden away behind its native sandstone walls. Your first stop should be the visitors information center at 1408 Ivinson Avenue in order to pickup a campus map and obtain a parking permit. Next, find your way to the **❖ Geological Museum** in the east wing of the S. H. Knight Geology Building. It is one of few such museums in the Rocky Mountains and its fossil exhibit rivals those in the eastern United States. In the 1960s Samuel H. Knight hand-hammered copper sheets into a lifesize Tyrannosaurus rex that now guards the entrance to the museum. Inside, a 70-foot-long skeleton of the Jurassic-period Apatosaurus excelsus (also known as Brontosaurus) is a must-see. It is the only Apatosaurus residing west of the Mississippi River and one of only five specimens on display worldwide. This 150-million-year-old fossil was discovered 70 miles north of Laramie in 1901. Overall, fifty types of dinosaurs have been unearthed in Wyoming. The museum has dozens of interpretive displays that tell the dinosaur story and the state's geological history. In prehistoric times Wyoming was covered by a sea and had a tropical climate. Recently an Allosaurus fossil was discovered near Shell, Wyoming, and will be displayed at the museum. The museum is open Monday through Friday from 8:00 A.M. to 5:00 P.M. and also on some weekends. Call 766–4218 for information.

Moving from fauna to flora, the **Rocky Mountain Herbarium** on campus represents one of the major plant collections in the nation. Located on the third floor of the Aven Nelson Memorial Building, the herbarium houses more than 540,000 dried plant specimens, including all of Wyoming's known flowering plants. It is the largest and most representative collection of Central Rocky Mountain plants anywhere. Although the herbarium is primarily a research facility, the general public may visit on Monday through Friday from 7:30 A.M. to 4:30 P.M. or by arrangement. Call 766–2236 for more information.

The University of Wyoming tour would not be complete without a stop at the **Insect Gallery** in room 4018 of the Agriculture Building. The collection, started more than one hundred years ago, features live displays of such creatures as hermit crabs, Madagascar hissing cockroaches, and tarantulas as well as thousands of mounted insects from all over the world. In all, the collection includes more than a quarter of a million insect specimens. The gallery is open Monday through Friday from 9:00 A.M. to noon and 1:00 to 4:00 P.M. To schedule a visit call 766–5338.

Being a university town, Laramie has its share of good restaurants and coffeehouses. One of our favorite eateries is ◆ **The Overland Restaurant,** located near the railroad tracks at 100 Ivinson Avenue. Prices are moderate and if you are fortunate enough to be in town on a weekend check out the wild game dinner special. The Overland also has a fine assortment of wines and beers, if you are so inclined. Call 721–2800 for information.

If you are looking for a secluded place to enjoy lunch during the warm-weather months, try **Jeffrey's Two** at 116 South Second Street. It features great sandwiches served in an inner courtyard away from the street traffic and Wyoming breezes. Call 742–0744. **Jeffrey's Bistro** around the corner at 123 Ivinson Avenue specializes in delicious desserts and fine dining. Prices are moderate. Call 742–7046.

Now, for that perfect cup of java or hot chocolate, mosey over to the **Coal Creek Coffee Company** at 110 Grand Avenue. The folks there also serve great muffins, scones, and soup. On the weekends the Coal Creek Coffee Company provides entertainment in the form of readings and what else but coffeehouse singers. Call 745–7737.

For a fine dining experience walk over to **Cafe Jacques** and enjoy a wide selection of innovative entrees in an elegant atmosphere, with cozy dining nooks, linen tablecloths, and artworks on display. Cafe Jacques is located at 216 Grand Avenue. For reservations call 742–5522. After catting-the-drag, drop in at the **Fabulous Fifties Diner** at 615 South Second Street and grab a great burger and shake or other fifties fare. Be sure to wear your jeans and poodle skirts and check out the yellow 1936 Oldsmobile in the middle of the restaurant. Call 742–5599.

For some nightlife get ready to line dance at **The Cowboy Saloon & Dance Hall** at 108 South Second Street. Warning: It's elbow-to-elbow crowded during the school year when the university students are in town, but it's always fun to watch or participate in the revelry. For information call 721–3165.

By now you have crisscrossed Ivinson Avenue at least a dozen times. The name comes from Edward and Jane Ivinson, Laramie's most prominent family. Edward Ivinson was a banker who built an elaborate Queen Anne–style mansion in 1892 in the expectation of using the residence as the Governor's House once he became elected to that office. The gesture was a grand expression of self-confidence not matched by public sentiment. In 1973 the then-abandoned home was converted into **The Laramie Plains Museum** at 603 Ivinson Avenue. Years of renovation have helped restore the structure to its former elegance. Among its collections are a well-outfitted kitchen with century-old appliances, a one-room schoolhouse located on the property, intricately hand-carved furniture made by prisoners at the Wyoming

Territorial Prison, and period clothing from wedding dresses to funeral wear. During the summer, the museum periodically sponsors "Tea on Tuesday" fund-raising events. Volunteers prepare scrumptious desserts and finger foods to accompany your tea or coffee while you enjoy a program based on the museum's collections and local history. There is a nominal fee for the docent-guided tour. For information on summer or winter schedules call 742–4448.

For the architecture buff, Laramie has a variety of architectural styles. Tour **Historic Downtown Laramie** between First and Third Sxtreets, extending from University Avenue to Garfield Street, to view landmark buildings dating from the 1800s. It's also a great chance to see the neat one-of-a-kind shops in Laramie. Start your tour with the 1910 **Elks Lodge Building** at 103 S. Second Street, which illustrates the Italianate style with a cornice supported by heavy brackets. **St. Matthews Cathedral** at 104 S. Fourth Street introduces a dignified old-English touch to the once rough-and-tumble end-of-tracks/hell-on-wheels town. The **Albany County Courthouse** exhibits Depression-era art deco style, at Grand Avenue and Sixth Street.

There are two styles of houses characteristic of railroad worker accommodations. In 1883 Theodore Bath constructed a row of seven small stone cottages, **Bath Row,** to rent to employees of the Union Pacific Railroad. They are among the oldest rental properties in Laramie. Several of the Bath Houses have been restored and are on the National Register of Historic Places. They are located on the east side of Sixth Street in block 100. The other style is the shotgun house, which we will visit later.

Notice the mixture of masonry styles in the brickwork of the Tudor Revival residence at 156 North Eighth Street. For an example of a pre-1872 Gothic Revival house, with gables, decorated with verge boards and finials at the peaks of the roof gables, travel to 310 South Tenth Street. The **University of Wyoming Alumni House** at 214 South Fourteenth Street is a fine example of Tudor Revival. The 1930s Art Moderne house at 1415 Custer Street features rounded corners and contrasting yellow and mauve brickwork exhibiting a frieze effect.

The 1921 **Cooper Mansion,** now the home of the University of Wyoming's American Studies program, at the corner of Grand Avenue and Fifteenth Street, combines the Mission and Pueblo

Laramie Plains Museum

Revival styles popular in southern California. Rich decorations, such as tiled fireplaces, decorative hardwood flooring, a grand staircase with carved balustrade and cypress beams imported from Europe, highlight the interior. Wilbur Hitchcock, a noted Laramie architect and designer of many University of Wyoming buildings, designed the mansion for Arthur F. T. Cooper, a wealthy English rancher who settled in Albany County. The Cooper Mansion can be viewed Monday through Friday from 8:00 A.M. to 5:00 P.M.

Travel to West Laramie for an example of the shotgun house, located at 154 Railroad Street. The shotgun style was originally one room wide, one story high, and usually two to four rooms deep. The entrance was on the gable end with the door and a window facing the street. Most Wyoming shotgun houses were built between the 1870s and 1920s as housing for Union Pacific workers. The name came about because you could fire a shotgun through the front door and the shot would emerge through the back door.

Conclude your tour at 810 East University Avenue at **Annie Moore's Guest House,** a well-restored Victorian home now serving as a bed and breakfast. It was built in 1910 by an early Laramie rancher. Later it housed the Delta Phi Sigma sorority and operated as Annie Moore's Boarding House from 1937 to 1948. It includes six antiques-furnished guest rooms and a delightful breakfast. Rooms run in the $50–$75 per night range. For information or reservations call 721–4177 or (800) 552–8992.

Before starting out on a loop tour of the nearby Snowy Range and historic Centennial, Saratoga, and Encampment, take a short ride to the remains of Fort Sanders on the southern outskirts of Laramie. In 1866 the federal government established Fort John Buford 3 miles south of present-day Laramie. The fort was later renamed Fort Sanders, after Brigadier General William P. Sanders, and enlarged to provide protection for travelers on the stage line from Denver to Salt Lake City and on the Overland Trail, both of which passed nearby. The post was abandoned in 1882 and in 1886 the Wyoming Territorial Legislature authorized the building of the first fish hatchery in Wyoming at old Fort Sanders. Unfortunately, all that is left is a partial wall and some foundations of the old fort. There is a marker within the fenced area surrounding the shell of the Fort Sanders guardhouse. Though not much remains of the fort, it is still a worthwhile trip. To view Fort Sanders take Third Street south out of town until it becomes Highway 287. Continue about a mile and a half and turn right onto South Kiowa Street. The structure is on your left a few hundred yards down the dirt road.

Fishing streams along the southeast portion of Wyoming are part of the Platte River drainage. Lake Hattie off Highway 230 is a good place to find rainbow and brown trout. For information on other good fishing spots, such as the Miracle Mile, contact Wyoming Game and Fish at 528 South Adams in Laramie or call 745–4046.

For today's excursion we suggest packing a picnic lunch to enjoy along with some breathtaking scenery. Take the Snowy Range Road (Highway 130) headed west out of Laramie toward

Centennial. Along the way you will view high-plains grasses, windswept basins, pine- and aspen-forested foothills, high mountain ranges with pristine glacial lakes, and more. Keep your eyes open for antelope herds, coyote, foxes, and mule deer. The **Snowy Range Scenic Byway** was designated as the second National Forest Service Byway in the nation in 1988. Built in the 1870s, it was originally a wagon road and was widened using horse-drawn equipment in the 1920s. Note: The portion through the Snowy Range a few miles after Centennial is open only from Memorial Day through October, weather permitting.

Ten miles out of Laramie there's a marker for the Overland Trail on the north (right) side of the road. In another 11 miles you'll reach the entrance to the ❖ **Vee Bar Guest Ranch** on the right. The original 1893 structure had its roof raised in 1912 with the addition of a second story. Over its hundred-year history, this Centennial Valley landmark served as a working cattle ranch, the Fillmore Stagecoach Stop, a boardinghouse, a buffalo ranch, and a year-round guest ranch.

Carla and Jim "Lefty" Cole and Sandy and C. L. Burton own the Vee Bar and have restored and preserved this Western gem. The barn is listed on the National Register of Historic Places. Activities include year-round horseback riding, hay wagon rides, skeet shooting, archery, overnight camp-outs, and river tubing. Great trout fishing is available on the ranch through its catch-and-release program. Riders of all skill levels will enjoy the horse excursions in the surrounding meadows and mountains. An extra-special true Western experience awaits you when you move the "doggies." Four cattle drives take place during the season; in addition some cattle are moved on a weekly basis.

Your schedule is flexible because you choose what activities you want to participate in during your stay. Nighttime entertainment takes a variety of forms, from historians to ventriloquists to cowboy poets to musicians leading a sing-along. Grab a seat by the fireplace and join in for a song or two.

The food is superb, varied, and served family style in the Western tradition. There's plenty of fresh vegetables and fruits and delicious homemade bread. As one guest remarked, "I've never been so cared for in my life."

For your accommodations, you can choose among a house in the meadows; cabins along and near the Little Laramie River, which meanders along the entire length of the ranch; or the new duplex suites built from logs recycled from 1890s homestead buildings from Lefty and Carla's Centennial Valley ranch. Your steps will echo as you walk along the lit boardwalk to the main ranch house.

From early June to early September, the Vee Bar Guest Ranch offers a variety of weekly accommodation packages starting at $3,595 per week. The rest of the year, guests can avail themselves of daily bed-and-breakfast rates and enjoy cross-country skiing, horseback riding, snowmobiling, or the nearby Snowy Range ski slopes. Winter bed-and-breakfast rates start at $100 per day. On Friday through Sunday you can also take advantage of an evening candlelight meal with a choice of seven menu items. For information and reservations call 745–7036 or (800) 4–VEE–BAR.

Seven miles down Highway 130, you run into the quaint, historic mining town of Centennial (population 100) at the base of the Snowy Range Mountains. Founded in 1875, Centennial owes its name to America's centennial year and its existence to the discovery of gold in "them thar hills." The promising vein soon played out and only the stalwarts remained to populate the rest stop for travelers on their way to the Snowies. The town's annual **Grass Roots Day** attracts visitors from far and wide on the last Saturday in July. The **Country Junction** on the eastern edge of town (you can see the whole town from this vantage point) has a good selection of hard candy and ice cream as well as unique and reasonably priced Western wear, antiques, and household decorations. The address is 2742 Highway 130, and the telephone number is 745–3318.

Don't let the small size of the 1907 railroad depot housing the **Nici Self Museum** discourage you from visiting. It's a great little museum within walking distance from the Country Junction. The structure is the oldest surviving depot of the Laramie, Hahn's Peak, and Pacific Railway Company originally formed to haul the large amounts of gold anticipated from the mountain mines. The historical collections contain exhibits on blacksmithing, lumbering, mining, railroading, and ranching. Outside, you'll find a beehive (wigwam) burner used to burn sawdust and a 1944 Union Pacific caboose. The museum is open from July 4 through Labor Day from 1:00 to 4:00 P.M. or by special appointment. For information call 742–7158.

On up the hill, **The Old Corral** is actually relatively new, having been rebuilt after a recent fire. The restaurant specializes in steaks, and rooms let for $40 for a single and $55 for a double year-round. Check out the unique woodwork in the bar area. Food prices are moderate. For more information and reservations call 745–5918 or (800) 678–2024.

The Forest Service Visitors Center a mile west of Centennial provides maps and information on the Snowies and the Medicine Bow National Forest, which you are now re-entering. You were also in part of the same forest near Vedauwoo, between Cheyenne and Laramie. For information on Medicine Bow National Forest call 745–2300.

About 32 miles west of Laramie the **Snowy Range Ski Area** provides affordable skiing for the whole family beginning in mid-November and lasting through mid-April, depending on snow conditions. The facilities include four lifts, twenty-three downhill trails, a network of cross-country trails, certified ski instruction, and a cafe and lounge. For information call 745–5750 or (800) GO-2-SNOW.

Two miles farther up the road, an entrepreneurial company has opened a new restaurant/lodge in the historic S. H. Knight Science Camp Buildings of the former University of the Wilderness. The **Snowy Mountain Lodge**, which opened in 1995, is nestled under the trees at 9,800 feet. The 1920s-vintage restaurant area, crafted out of logs, is unique in that it has a tree trunk rising through the floor and ceiling.

There are thirteen restored rustic cabins for overnight guests. Cabin rates are $35 and up per night. The restaurant is open from 8:00 A.M. to 9:00 P.M. daily with variations for hunting season and winter season. Prices are moderate to expensive, and you can choose from a variety of steak, fish, and chicken dinner entrees. There are a number of hiking and cross-country ski trails on the property, which has several streams running through it. For added adventure, since the Wyoming Highway Department does not snowplow the road to the lodge in the winter, the lodge will bring people from the main road to the lodge via a snowcat machine capable of carrying up to ten people at once. For information and reservations call 742–SNOW.

The highest point on the Snowy Range Road is at Libby Flats, 10,000 feet above sea level. Medicine Bow Peak at 12,013 towers over Libby Flats. The **Libby Observation Point** scenic outlook

offers a breathtaking vista of alpine meadows and several mountain ranges in Wyoming and Colorado. The area abounds with off-
the-road trails, campgrounds, and lakes stocked with trout, and an
incredible variety of wildflowers can be found on the Libby Flats
Wildflower Trail. You can locate patches of snow in this area even
during the peak temperatures of August. Bring a sweater because
the altitude and cold winds will bring a chill to your bones.

CARBON COUNTY

The best is yet to come. Follow Snowy Ridge Road as it winds
west from the summit at Libby Flats until you come to the splendor of **Mirror Lake** and ◆ **Lake Marie.** Now is the time to
bring out the picnic basket, as you sit on the rocks at the shore of
Lake Marie and gaze into its crystal-clear waters. The trailhead for
Medicine Bow Peak originates at Lake Marie with its dramatic
backdrop of glacial formations reaching skyward.

Push on west until you come to North Brush Creek Road (Fire
Ranger Road 100) and turn right. This will lead you to the top of
Kennaday Peak (formerly called Bald Mountain or Old Baldy),
named after an early homesteader and ranger. A flight of stairs gets
you into the 14-foot-square glass room of the **Kennaday Peak
Lookout.** From your vantage point far above the treeline you
get a panorama of spectacular views. The lookout tower is open
Friday through Tuesday from 10:00 A.M. to 5:00 P.M., weather permitting. Slippery road conditions may exist after a rain or snow.
For information call the Brush Creek Visitors Center at 326–5562
or the Forest Service Saratoga District Office at 326–5258.

Retrace your tracks back to Highway 130 and head west until
you reach Highway 230, then head south 10 miles and turn onto
Highway 70 until you hit Encampment (population 490). Native
Americans gathered at Camp le Grand or Grand Encampment,
situated at the base of the Sierra Madre Mountains, in order to
hunt buffalo and other wild game. Later, trappers rendezvoused
in the area. In the late 1880s the area grew into a productive
copper-mining district after Ed Haggarty made a large strike on
the Continental Divide near Bridger Peak. Once proclaimed the
"Copper Capital of the United States," Encampment had the
longest aerial tramway in the world. Built in 1902, it conveyed
copper ore 16 miles from the famous Rudefeha Mine (named

after the four original partners: Rumsey, Deal, Ferris, and Haggarty), or Ferris-Haggarty Mine, to the smelter at Encampment. Power was supplied by water through a 4-foot-wide wooden pipeline. The original partners were bought out by a Chicago promoter, and the name of the mining company changed to North American Copper Company. Millions of dollars of copper were shipped out of Encampment before the price of copper collapsed in 1908. The mines closed and the owner was indicted for overcapitalization and fradulent stock sales.

The excellent ◆ **Grand Encampment Museum** has been around for some thirty years and can keep you prowling around its intriguing displays for hours. First of all, there's the two-story outhouse that solved the problem of contending with the deep winter snow. Then there's the folding oak bathtub. Well, you get the idea. The museum grounds feature numerous historic buildings, such as a tie hack's cabin, livery stable, false-front store, newspaper office, and stage station, as well as part of the 16-mile aerial tramway. The Grand Encampment Museum is located at Seventh and Barnett streets, although street signs are hard to find in Encampment. You can also pick up a map for the tour of **Historic Homes of Grand Encampment** at the museum. The museum is open daily from Memorial Day Weekend through Labor Day from 1:00 to 5:00 P.M. and on weekends September through October or by appointment. Call 327–5308 for information.

To take a real look at frontier life, time your visit for the annual **Woodchoppers Jamboree and Rodeo** held at Encampment in mid-June. The event lasts two days and includes lumbering competitions with lumberjacks arriving from as far away as California and Australia. Watch skilled ax throwers whiz axes through the air to their intended target while you enjoy a delicious barbecue. Call Grand Encampment Museum at 327–5308 for information on the jamboree.

You might entertain the thought of some side excursions from Encampment. Of course, the nearby Sierra Madre copper-mining **Ghost Towns of Dillon and Rudefeha** beckon. Both have remnants of the buildings and mining equipment that made these towns bustling settlements. Inquire locally about directions and road conditions, and if a four-wheel-drive vehicle is required. Many roads passable in dry weather frequently turn into a quagmire after a rain.

If you are up to an hour-long hike, we advise striking out on the **Indian Bathtubs Trail** to see the natural 4-foot-deep depressions in granite rock formations, which were used by Native Americans for bathing. You can obtain information and maps at the Encampment–Riverside Merchants Association or Riverside Visitors Center, or call 327–5265. To reach the area from Riverside take Highway 230 east 1 mile to Carbon County Road 200. Turn south on that road, also known as Blackhail Mountain Road, and proceed 1 mile to a parking area. Follow the trail, which travels in a southwesterly direction. The trail crosses a sagebrush flat and then proceeds up an incline to a bench at the halfway mark. It then crosses a rocky ridge before a fairly steep descent to Cottonwood Creek. The round trip should take about one hour, and good hiking boots are advisable. From the vantage point of the bathtubs you obtain a good view of the entire Medicine Bow Mountain Range and the Encampment-Riverside Valley.

Eighteen miles north of Encampment, you can relax your body in the warm mineral springs by the North Platte River in Saratoga. The average temperature of the mineral water is 114 degrees Fahrenheit. The **Hobo Pool** is free and open twenty-four hours every day of the year. It is located at the east end of Walnut Street. The town was originally called Warm Springs and was renamed in 1884 after the famed Saratoga Springs resort area in New York State.

Stop in at the historic ◆ **Hotel Wolf** built in 1893 and used as a stagecoach stop on the Encampment-to-Walcott stage line. The Victorian atmosphere and antique-decorated rooms transport one back a century in time. The food is excellent and moderate to expensive in price. The restaurant has earned a prestigious triple diamond rating from the American Automobile Association. Hotel Wolf is listed on the National Register of Historic Places. The hotel is located at 101 East Bridge Street. Call 326–5525 for information.

For lighter fare stop in at **Lollypops** one door down at 107 East Bridge Street. This charming place features great croissants, Belgian waffles, soups, sandwiches, ice cream, and nonfat yogurt.

Spend some time visiting Saratoga's fine art gallaries and Whitney's Platte Valley Mercantile. The **Rustic Bar** at 124 East Bridge Street displays some impressive stuffed wildlife, including two mountain lions above the back bar, two bucks with their antlers locked together in a life-and-death struggle, and a whimsical scene of chipmunks and prairie dogs frequenting a bar.

The **Saratoga Museum** is located across from the airport at 104 Constitution Avenue in an original 1915 Union Pacific Railroad depot. The Saratoga Historical and Cultural Association sponsors guided tours to various local historical landmarks during the summer, and for a small fee you can join these excursions. Museum displays include Native American tools and weapons, railroad memorabilia, and Platte Valley artifacts. The museum is open Memorial Day to Labor Day from 1:00 to 5:00 P.M. For information call 326–5511.

Saratoga is known as the town where "trout leap on Main Street." The North Platte River, which flows through town, is designated as a blue-ribbon trout stream by the Wyoming Game and Fish Department for approximately 65 miles from where the river enters the state and flows northward through Saratoga to where Sage Creek enters the river. It attracts anglers from far and wide. The annual February **Donald E. Erickson Memorial Cutter Races** and **Saratoga Draft Horse Pull** are great winter events to watch. For information call Saratoga–Platte Valley Chamber of Commerce at 326–8855.

Heading back toward Laramie on Highway 130, turn south on Carbon County Highway 203 for a stay at ✦ **Brush Creek Ranch.** The ranch entrance is a mile down the road on the left side. Brush Creek is a working cattle ranch and encompasses 6,000 acres. It has been family owned for four generations. Choose your accommodations from the many rooms in the 7,000-square-foot main ranch house, built in the early 1900s and expanded in the 1930s. Or perhaps one of the renovated Western-decorated cabins would suit you better. Sit on the peaceful veranda of the main house as the sun sets behind the Sierra Madre Mountains.

You will find plenty to do, such as horseback riding, hayrides, hiking, campfires and cookouts, cross-country skiing, and barn dances in the old loft. Kids eight and under have an exciting and informative time with the wranglers in the corrals. Of course, you are invited to help out with the ranch chores, such as branding, mending fences, and rounding up cattle. "On Mondays we meet with the guests to get them to think like a cow. It readies them for the real cattle moving," says ranch manager Dieter

Greiner. For those interested in quality fishing, Brush Creek Ranch is an Orvis-endorsed lodge, one of only two in Wyoming.

Flower gardens bloom around the property and a fountain from the 1920s flows nearby. Robber's Roost, a rock outcropping used as a hideaway by a band of bank robbers who had looted nearby Encampment, looms behind the main ranch house.

Guests enjoy generous meals in the vintage Western mural-decorated dining room and then lounge around the quartz fireplace. It's a great place to relax and live the West. Weekly rates start at $1,025. For information call 327–5241 or (800) 726–2499, or write to Brush Creek Ranch, Star Route 10, Saratoga 82331.

The northerly road out of Laramie puts you on Highway 30, the original Lincoln Highway route to Medicine Bow. About 18 miles northwest out of Laramie, Highway 34 angles off to the right (east) to the **Wyoming Game and Fish Department Sybille Canyon Wildlife Research and Visitors Center** (about a 26-mile round-trip). It is home to a breeding and re-introduction program for black-footed ferrets, plus a short nature walk and picnic area. The center is open April 1 through November 15 from 8:30 A.M. to 4:30 P.M.

The black-footed ferret, once prevalent on most Wyoming prairies, was considered virtually extinct owing to disease until a number were captured in the mid-1980s. The ferrets were separated into three groups to prevent disease from wiping out the remaining population. Seven ferrets were sent to a branch of the National Zoo near Washington, D.C., eight journeyed to the Henry Doorly Zoo in Omaha, Nebraska, and the rest took up residence at the Sybille Research facility in Wyoming. Since then, more than 240 ferrets have been bred in captivity and a number have been reintroduced into the wilderness of the Shirley Basin and are being closely monitored. Other black-footed ferrets have been sent to various captive breeding programs at zoos in Arizona, Colorado, Kentucky, and Canada.

Rejoining Highway 30, the next stop is Rock River (population 190), which is 21 miles northwest of Bosler and a few miles outside Carbon County, in Albany County. Be sure to stop in at the **Rock River Museum** to get a look at the safe blown up in the famous June 2, 1899, Wilcox train robbery by Butch Cassidy and his band of outlaws. As legend has it, four masked men stopped the Union Pacific train. They pounded on the door of the express car and demanded entrance. But the expressman refused to open the door. Being a bit impatient, the highwaymen placed a stick of dynamite into the door and set it off. As shown in the movie *Butch Cassidy and the Sundance Kid,* the explosion demolished the railcar. More dynamite had to be used to open the safe before the Wild Bunch made off with $55,000.

The museum is located in the old First National Bank, which went out of business in 1927. Other interesting exhibits around the museum are dinosaur fossils, mineral displays, Rock River memorabilia, and photographs of the nearby ghost town of Rock Creek, a major cattle shipping point until the railroad rerouted its track in 1900 through Rock River. You can still find a few buildings, such as the Rock Creek pump house, standing at the ghost town site about 8 miles north of Rock River. The Rock River Museum is located at 131 Avenue C. It is open Memorial Day through Labor Day on Wednesday through Sunday from noon to 5:00 P.M. Call 378–2205 for information.

Continuing on Highway 30 for approximately 9 miles you arrive at the **Como Bluffs Fossil Cabin** and step back in time millions of years. The odd-looking structure on the right-hand side of the road was featured in "Ripley's Believe It or Not" as the oldest building in the world. It was constructed of dinosaur bones found in the area. Como Bluffs is the site of a major dinosaur discovery in 1877 and supplier to major dinosaur exhibits in museums around the world. Yale paleontologist Othniel Charles Marsh and his rival Edward Drinker Cope of the Philadelphia Academy of Sciences fought over the bones, sabotaged each other's excavations, and quarreled bitterly through the press for years. Although most of the quarry work was finished decades ago, a recent discovery of a previously unknown species of the Brontosaurus family in the Como Bluffs area has sparked renewed interest. Unfortunately, the Fossil Cabin is closed and in disrepair.

Once again we enter Carbon County as we approach Medicine Bow (population 389), located 18 miles northwest of Rock River. The sleepy town is perhaps one of the most well known in all of the West. It was the setting for Owen Wister's landmark Western novel *The Virginian.* The classic phrase from the novel, "When you call me that, smile," reportedly originated in Medicine Bow during a poker game in which the Carbon County deputy sheriff

was called a less than flattering name. Wister, gathering local flavor for his novel, overheard the deputy sheriff's retort and made
Medicine Bow and the phrase famous.

Despite its size, Medicine Bow boasts two sites listed on the
National Register of Historic Places: the ✦ **Virginian Hotel**
(opened in 1911, nine years after publication of the novel) and
the 1913 Union Pacific Depot, which houses a fine museum.
The **Medicine Bow Museum** is located across Highway 30
from the Virginian Hotel and is open during the summer
months, and hunting season, and part-time during the winter.
Call 379–2383 for hours.

The museum contains plenty of interesting Western and local
artifacts, including the blackjack table from the Medicine Bow
Casino. The Owen Wister Cabin (used by Wister as a summer
home and winter hunting lodge) and Owen Wister Monument
(made out of petrified wood) are located next to the museum.
The Owen Wister General Store is the actual building where he
slept on the counter upon arriving in Medicine Bow in 1885.
Another interesting exhibit, **"The Brands That Tamed the
West,"** is situated adjacent to the museum.

The Virginian Hotel had the first electric lights in Medicine Bow.
At the time it was the largest hotel between Denver and Salt Lake
City and the site of business dealings, romance, and a few shootings. A Grand Reopening in 1984 marked the restoration of the
hotel's turn-of-the-century Victorian decor. Inside there's a lunch
counter with a great old Western mural on the wall where the
locals gather, and the Owen Wister Dining Room serves good food
at moderate prices. The hotel's Shiloh Saloon is another favorite
meeting spot for locals and travelers alike. Accommodations
include rooms with a shared bath for $20 a night, small suites for
$35 per night, and the spacious Owen Wister Suite with two bed-
rooms, a sitting room, and a massive brass bed for $65 per night.
For information call 379–2377.

Every July the town celebrates **Medicine Bow Days,** complete with a bull-chip-throwing contest, dancing, melodrama, a
rodeo, and the Hanging of Dutch Charlie at High Noon. Dutch
Charlie and Big Nose George were suspected of killing two
deputies. Dutch Charlie met his fate at Old Carbon, a ghost town
14 miles southwest of Medicine Bow. We'll learn more about the

unusual fate of Big Nose George later. For dates and information call 379–2571.

The Arapahoe and Cheyenne discovered excellent material for making their wooden bows along the banks of the river. They called the wood "good medicine" and named the river Medicine Bow. In the early 1870s the town became a major supply point for forts in Wyoming and the government established a military post in Medicine Bow to protect the railroad and freight wagons from Indian attack.

The federal government returned to the area in 1982 in attempts to harness the Medicine Bow wind with the construction of the **World's Largest Wind Turbine.** Rising like a phoenix out of the high plains, the 262-foot WTS–4 still commands the skyline with unchallenged authority even though the feds abandoned the wind project in 1986, after spending millions of dollars on the experiment. In 1989 a modern-day Don Quixote purchased the broken wind turbine from a government garage sale for $20,000. Over the next few years, retired engineer Don Young dared to "dream the impossible dream," spending fifteen-hour days and a small sum of money to get the wind turbine back in operation (the government had received bids of $1 million to replace the generator and $200,000 for removal and repair of the generator). A trial run in February/March 1992 proved a disappointment and Young went back to the drawing boards with the help of an associate and $60,000 in capital. This time, hard work and patience paid off. By Thanksgiving of 1992, Young got the wind turbine up and running. Over the next few months, the electricity it generated was sold to the Western Area Power Authority, allowing Young and his partner to recoup their investment. Unfortunately, the pitch control system of the WTS–4 went awry in early 1994, causing the blade to hit the tower and shatter. The tower of the world's largest wind turbine can be seen on the southwest horizon from Medicine Bow.

Follow Highway 30 as it turns southwest. Nineteen miles later you will find the entrance to Hanna (population 1,076), which has a long history of coal mining. The community was named after Marcus Hanna, the Cleveland, Ohio, industrialist and U.S. senator. The vast coal deposits were discovered in 1886, and a **Miners Monument** memorializes the 228 miners who died during mine explosions in 1903 and 1908. To locate the monument follow the signs at the eastern edge of town.

If you are in the mood for a cooling swim, the **Hanna Recreation Center** at 8000 Highway 72 has an inviting swimming pool and whirlpool for use at a modest fee. A newer Miners Monument and a Union Pacific snowplow engine are located near the center. For information and hours call 325-9402.

At this point take Highway 72 south 12 miles to Elk Mountain for a real treat. The town of 186 gets its name from nearby Elk Mountain (elevation 11,167). Mike McCarthy, storekeeper of the **◆ Elk Mountain Trading Company,** is an interesting fellow and is more than willing to chew the fat for a bit. According to Mike, the Elk Mountain Trading Post once grubstaked a rancher who later amassed a fortune of $78 million. The trading post has all sorts of antiques scattered about the place, along with some king-size bear traps. There's also the Noon Camp Cafe in the building and, if you're in luck, a fresh batch of delicious sugar cookies will beckon from the oven.

"People stop in here all the time to get off Interstate 80 for a while and regain their sanity. We'll stay open to serve people as long as they want to stay," says McCarthy. To check if the Elk Mountain Trading Company and Noon Camp Cafe are open, call 348-7478.

Exit off Interstate 80 about 25 miles west of Elk Mountain to view the site of **◆ Fort Fred Steele.** After a look at the sagebrush countryside, you might wonder how a soldier in his right mind might accept an assignment at this desolate outpost. The answer, of course, is that orders were orders and there wasn't much room for negotiation in the calvary. In fact, Fort Fred Steele gained the dubious reputation of possessing the highest desertion rate of any post in the West.

Named after Union Civil War hero Major General Frederick Steele, the post was established in 1868 to protect Overland Trail and Union Pacific Railroad traffic. A Union Pacific line still runs through the fort site. The 1881 brick powder magazine remains, as do the foundations of many buildings from the original fort. Civilians took over the buildings after the government abandoned the fort in 1886. The railroad-tie business kept the fledgling town alive and it even enjoyed a brief spurt when the original Lincoln Highway route went right through the town. By the 1930s, the town was all but dried up. A few hangers-on still live there today. The restored 1880s **Bridge Tender House** now serves as an interpretive center. The fort is administered by the State of Wyoming as a state historic site. Summer hours are May 1 to September 15 from 9:00 A.M. to 7:00 P.M. There are no overnight camping facilities but there are picnic areas where you can watch the action of the North Platte River. For information call 328–0115.

Another 9 miles down the interstate you come upon a picturesque little town called **Sinclair** (population 500). The Sinclair oil refinery at the edge of town gives away the story behind the town's name. Back during the oil boom of the twenties, however, the company town sprung up as Parco, built by and named after the Producers Oil and Refining Company. Designed in Spanish Mission style, the town includes a town square with a large fountain in front of the ❖ **Parco Inn,** which has been closed and abandoned for many years. Amelia Earhart, President Franklin Roosevelt, and union leader John L. Lewis all stayed at the Parco Inn. It once provided shelter to travelers on the bustling Lincoln Highway, which passed in front of the hotel, but both have since faded into history. Every few years or so, some well-intentioned dreamers announce plans to renovate and reopen the Parco Inn but they, too, soon fade into oblivion.

The Sinclair Oil Company purchased the refinery in 1934, and citizens voted to change the town's name from Parco to Sinclair in 1943. Although the Parco Inn closed its doors, there's still plenty of reason to stop off for an hour or two. The First National Bank of Parco operated from 1924 to 1933 in a building that now houses the **Sinclair/Parco Museum,** which has a rich collection of town and oil-refining artifacts. The museum is open year-round. If the museum door is locked, inquire about entrance at the Parco City Hall next door. Then, if you want some of the finest Mexican food in the West, follow Lincoln Avenue west until you see the **Mi Casa Cafe.** You'll be glad you did. Prices are inexpensive to moderate. For information call 789–9690 or 789–8733.

Twenty-seven miles north of Sinclair on Seminole Road (Road 351) you'll come upon **Seminole State Park,** designated in 1965 around the reservoir created with the construction of the Seminole Dam in 1939. The reservoir has 180 miles of shoreline, camping facilities, and great trout and walleye fishing. For park information call 328–0115.

Back in Sinclair, jump on Interstate 80 for 1 mile and exit at Rawlins, home of the ❖ **Wyoming Frontier Prison,** constructed in 1898 and active until 1982. A tour through the old cell blocks brings a chill to one's spine, as does a visit to the gas chamber (round-trip, fortunately). Among notable prisoners who served time at the Rawlins facility were Annie Bruce, who murdered her father with a poisoned plum pie; William Carlisle, the last great train robber; Talton Taylor, the last man hanged by the State of Wyoming, in 1933; and Perry H. Carroll, the first man executed by the gas chamber in Wyoming, in 1937. The oldest man buried in the old prison cemetery was Jim Best, who died of natural causes at age eighty-nine. Best had been released after serving his time. He was given the standard new suit, $15 in cash, and a sack lunch. He enjoyed his lunch on the lawn of the prison and then returned to the gate and asked to be readmitted. He died shortly after. Guided tours are provided Memorial Day weekend through Labor Day weekend seven days a week from 8:30 A.M. to 6:30 P.M. and during the off season by appointment. There's a great book written by an inmate of the prison, titled *The Sweet Smell of Sagebrush,* available at the prison gift shop. The native sandstone, castlesque Wyoming Frontier Prison is located at Fifth and Walnut Streets. For information call 324–4422.

The town was named after General John A. Rawlins, chief of staff of the U.S. Army, who discovered a spring at the base of the hills in 1867. The spot was called Rawlins Springs, later shortened to Rawlins, and the town sprung up where the Union Pacific Railroad divided 20 miles east of the Continental Divide. The **Carbon County Museum** at Ninth and Walnut Streets contains a number of interesting exhibits, including the death mask and shoes made from the skin of notorious outlaw Big Nose George, sheep wagons originating in Rawlins, and a fine assortment of arrowheads and Native American pottery.

Big Nose George was an outlaw and murderer. Asked why he had killed two deputies, Big Nose answered, "On the principle that dead men tell no tales." Sentenced to hang on April 2, 1881, Big Nose attempted an escape from his cell a week before that date. News of the escape attempt made the rounds in Rawlins and a swarm of armed men broke into the jail, hauled Big Nose to a telegraph pole, and hanged him. No charges were ever brought against any members of the lynching party, who wore masks to hide their faces. A newly arrived doctor, John Osborne (elected governor of Wyoming in 1892), took charge of Big Nose's body. Legend has it that the enterprising doctor removed the outlaw's skin, tanned it, and made a pair of two-tone shoes. Doc Osborne put the rest of George's remains in a whiskey barrel and buried them behind his office on Cedar Street, where they were uncovered in 1950. Call 324–9611 for dates and hours of operation of the Carbon County Museum.

The **Rawlins Uplift** is one of the state's oldest geological formations and is certainly worth a look. You'll find it north of town. The Rawlins Uplift outlines the eastern edge of the Great Divide Basin, the western end of southeastern Wyoming, and the beginning of the desert basins to the west. For the geologically inclined, Precambrian rocks are exposed in the core of the uplift and its flanks are composed of outwardly-dipping Paleozoic and Mesozoic strata. All in all, they are quite old rocks.

Try the great scones with honey butter served at the **Pantry Restaurant** at 221 West Cedar Street. If you need more substantial fare, stay for a complete meal. Prices are moderate and the sandwiches and dinners are excellent. Hours are from 7:00 A.M. to 9:00 P.M. For reservations call 324–7860.

For a pleasant evening and good breakfast, stay in the **Ferris Mansion,** listed on the National Register of Historic Places. The three-story brick Queen Anne–style Victorian mansion was designed by the Knoxville, Tennessee, firm of Barber and Klutz in 1903. The home was built by Julia Ferris, whose husband, George Ferris, had been killed in 1901 by a runaway team of horses as he was returning from his copper mine (the Haggarty-Ferris Mine) in the Grand Encampment Mining District. The restored mansion features a player piano in the parlor, a grand stairway, and comfortable sitting rooms. All rooms have private baths and televisions. Rooms are in the $50 to $75 range. The Ferris Mansion Bed and Breakfast is located at 607 West Maple Street. For reservations call 324–3961.

SWEETWATER COUNTY

Interstate 80 leaving Rawlins goes through the stark but beautiful red desert region, which is loaded with wild horses. Take the Continental Divide exit west of Creston Junction and cross under

Interstate 80 to find the secluded ❖ **Henry B. Joy Monument.**
Joy was president of the Packard Motor Company and a major
force in the Lincoln Highway movement as the first president of the
Lincoln Highway Association. The 1939 monument is surrounded
by a fence anchored by four concrete Lincoln Highway markers.

Journey another 51 miles down the road and you will find the
Point of Rocks Monument and ruins of the **Almond Overland Stage Station** south of the highway. This station also
served the South Pass City Route after gold was discovered in
that region. The sandstone station was built in 1862 when
"Stagecoach King" Ben Holladay moved his stage line south from
the Oregon Trail to the Overland Trail because of Indian hostili-
ties. The railroad replaced the need for the station and it was
abandoned in 1868. For a time, infamous Jack Slade served as
stationmaster. His violent temper caused the deaths of several
men and Slade eventually met his end at the end of a rope supplied by a Montana lynch mob.

Take Highway 371 north 7 miles along the drainage of Horse
Thief Creek to **Superior** (population 273) and discover a real
ghost town. At its peak, Superior boasted of 3,000 people drawn
by work in the underground coal mines. The most interesting
site is the ❖ **1921 Union Hall,** once teeming with labor activity and social events. All that exists today is the shell of the building. Built in the shape of a trapezoid, the remaining walls of the
once-impressive Union Hall building stand as a stark monument
to the boom-and-bust cycles of Wyoming's mining economy. In
forty years of mining activity more than twenty-three million
tons of coal were extracted from Superior area mines.

Get back on Interstate 80 and exit on Highway 191 North
Drive 3 miles and turn right onto Reliance Road. Here, another
strong testimonial to the volatility of the coal-mining industry
and the hard life of coal miners is the abandoned ❖ **Reliance
Tipple,** located northeast of Rock Springs. The Union Pacific
Coal Company built the town of Reliance in the first decade of
the twentieth century to house workers for the company's nearby
coal mines. The Reliance Tipple, one of only a few historic coal
tipples remaining in the state, was one of the largest and most
mechanically advanced coal tipples in Wyoming. Built in 1936,
the steel-and-iron tipple and the men, women, and children who
worked there sorted millions of tons of coal by size for loading

into waiting railroad cars. Interpretive signs around the tipple site provide a twenty-minute self-guided tour.

The ◆ **Natural History Museum** at Western Wyoming Community College in Rock Springs is a real treat. The museum's collections include interesting exhibits of Mayapan, Guatemalan, and Peruvian artifacts, such as water gourds, baskets, sling stones, blowguns, poison-dart quivers, and serpentine masks. The major attractions, however, are the full-size skeleton casts of dinosaurs located throughout the campus complex. A self-guided tour brochure obtained at the college information desk directs you to each dinosaur and gives a detailed description of it and a history of where and how it lived. A Triceratops greets you at the main campus entrance while a Camptosaurus guards the entrance to the bookstore. Triceratops looked like a gigantic rhinoceros and weighed up to six tons. It existed off giant palm fronds and leafy plants growing in then-swampy Wyoming. The original Triceratops from which the cast was made was found in eastern Wyoming near Lance Creek in 1889.

The Tyrannosaurus rex hovering over the student center is delicately balanced on two contact points. More than 80 million years ago, it roamed on the hills and among the gigantic rocks that serve as a backdrop to the display. There are only six T. rexes on display in the United States.

Search out the other interesting exhibits, including a miner's coal car, cave art, a replica of an Easter Island statue, a fossil man, and a Foucault pendulum. Located in the atrium of the student center, the pendulum continuously swings in the same plane. As the earth rotates, the room in which you stand rotates with it, but the pendulum is free. While it looks as if the pendulum moves with each motion, it is the room that has changed position owing to the rotation of the earth. The polished white granite slab over which the pendulum swings came from the Wind River Range and is estimated to have cooled down from its molten state more than 2.65 billion years ago. The green stone surrounding the granite was cut from a giant jade boulder discovered near Jeffrey City.

The Western Wyoming Community College is located at 2500 College Drive. The museum is open during campus hours, from 9:00 A.M. to 10:00 P.M. School vacation periods may affect the schedule. For information call 382–1666 or 382–1600.

We advise taking in **Historic Downtown Rock Springs** using the self-guided walking-tour pamphlet published by the Sweetwater County Joint Travel and Tourism Board. Copies are available at the Rock Springs Chamber of Commerce office at the intersection of Dewar and Firestone Roads, a few blocks from the Dewar Road exit off Interstate 80. For information call 362–3771.

The tour begins at the **Rock Springs Historic Museum** at the corner of Broadway and B Streets. You can visit the museum at the beginning or end of the tour—either way it is an enjoyable experience. The building was built in 1894 as the Rock Springs City Hall and was used in that capacity until a new City Hall was constructed in 1978. The museum opened in 1988 as part of Rock Springs' centennial celebrations. The elaborate Richardson Romanesque stone structure is listed on the National Register of Historic Places and represents the only example of that style of architecture remaining in southwestern Wyoming. It was completely restored in 1992. Its collections cover Rock Springs history from the early 1880s through the present. They include exhibits on coal mining and this "City of Fifty-six Nationalities." The Rock Springs Historical Museum is located at 201 B Street. Call 362–3138 for days and hours of operation.

The building at 440 South Main Street is one of the most interesting in Rock Springs with its distinctive stonework and roofline. The cut-sandstone exterior is only a facade, as the building structure is composed of brick. See if you can find the disappearing 1892 date carved into the stone. Using the guide, you can seek out other historic and interesting Rock Springs buildings.

Rock Springs gets its name from a spring discovered in the early 1860s, resulting in the establishment of a stage station along the Overland Trail. The town boomed when the Union Pacific tapped the area's large coalfields for fuel to run its trains. Ironically, the spring disappeared with the onset of coal mining. Despite Rock Springs' pride in being settled by fifty-six different nationalities, its history is scarred by the 1885 Chinese Massacre, brought on when Union Pacific introduced Chinese workers to replace white workers. As many as thirty Chinese workers were killed in the uprising, and federal troops were brought in. As reparation to the Chinese government, the U.S. government later funded scholarships for Chinese students in the United States.

For a bit of local flavor search out **Grubs** at 415 Paulson Street. You'll probably have to stand several deep at the horseshoe counter before you get served, but the hamburgers (called Shamrocks) and malts are great and the food is inexpensive. **The Park Grill** at 19 Elk Street specializes in Italian and American food. It's located in the historic Park Hotel and has been furnished with an art deco touch. The food prices are moderate. Call 362–3701. Two supper clubs located west of Rock Springs are also worth a try for delicious steaks and other entrees: the **Log Inn** (362–7166) and **White Mountain Mining Company** (382–5265). Prices at both restaurants are moderate to expensive.

If you are looking for a quiet place to stay and a great breakfast, Darlene Schertzer of the ◆**Sha Hol Dee B&B** at 1116 Pilot Butte Avenue in Rock Springs is a gracious host and fantastic cook. Nightly rates run in the $50 to $75 range. There are only three bedrooms, so make your reservations early.

Several miles north on Highway 191 out of Rock Springs, take Chilton Road (Road 17) through an intriguing land of ancient volcanoes and massive sand dunes. Use caution since these roads are definitely backcountry, with no services and few inhabitants. The ◆**Killpecker Dune Field** is the largest sand dune on the North American continent and second in size only to the Sahara Desert. It features an off-road vehicle area for those so inclined. The Killpecker Dune Field is home to a herd of rare desert elk found nowhere else in North America.

The remains of volcanoes can be seen as flat-topped buttes, including Black Rock, Boars Tusk, and North and South Table Mountain. **White Mountain** to the west of Chilton Road contains petroglyphs dating from the seventeenth to early nineteenth centuries.

After an hour or two in the desert you will probably be craving an ice cream cone, so stop at the **Farson Mercantile** at the crossroads of Highways 191 and 28 for the best deal in Wyoming. For 50 cents you receive a mammoth scoop of ice cream and for a dollar you get more ice cream than you can eat before the Wyoming sun melts it.

The California and Oregon Trails are located north on Highway 191. Just northeast of Farson is the "Parting of the Ways", where pioneers opted for one of two routes of the Oregon Trail. The shorter Sublette Cutoff went over more treacherous territory and the most difficult river crossing along the entire Oregon Trail. The cutoff received its name from William Sublette, who appears to have been the first white man to travel the route, in 1826. Its gentle descent from Steed Canyon on the east bank of the Green River allowed wagons a deceptively easy approach to the river. In June and early July, when emigrant wagons would have been attempting the crossing, they were met with high, swift water fed by the snowmelt. Mountain man Jim Bridger took advantage of the dangerous situation, establishing a profitable fee-based ferry system. The Mormons also operated a ferry system nearby at Names Hill, so-called because of the many early pioneers, including Jim Bridger, who carved their names into the sandstone rock face.

A trail register kept by emigrant Winfield Scott Espy describes his arrival at the ferry camp in 1854:

> . . . found as the saying is "all sorts of people" American traders, Frenchmen, Mormons, Loafers, Dandies, Gamblers, Idlers, Grog shopkeepers, Half Breeds & whole Breed Snake Indians . . . Boasting & bragging the order of the day as well as whiskey drinking & an occasional rowe . . .

The longer route passed southwest to Fort Bridger before swinging northwest to meet the Sublette Cutoff near present-day Cokeville.

Take Highway 191 South out of Rock Springs to arrive at the magnificent ◆ **Flaming Gorge National Recreation Area,** which flows over into Utah. The reservoir extends for 91 miles and provides ample recreational activities, from camping to fishing to waterskiing and river floating in the summer to cross-country skiing and snowmobiling in the winter. There's a gorgeous view from the Red Canyon Visitors Center at the north end of the dam, and you can travel completely around the Flaming Gorge Reservoir for a 160-mile journey following Highways 191, 260, 44, and 530 for a loop tour starting at Rock Springs and ending at Green River. Be on the alert for bighorn sheep, elk, moose, mule deer, and pronghorn antelope.

There are more than six hundred camping and picnic sites and hundreds of miles of hiking trails to enjoy. The Firehole Canyon recreation site on the east side of the reservoir provides easy access to fantastic high desert country vistas. There are a number of Flaming Gorge interpretive programs; inquire about them at the visitors centers. Most facilities are open from mid-May to mid-September and the route is open year-round, but travel at the higher elevations in the winter can be dangerous. To reserve a camping site at any of the Flaming Gorge National Recreation Area locations call (800) 280–CAMP.

Highway 530 lands you in Green River, home to **Expedition Island** where Major John Wesley Powell began his famous exploration of the Green and Colorado rivers in 1869. A plaque in the center of Expedition Island (Green River Island Park) commemorates the spot where Powell embarked on his journey.

Notes from the diaries kept by men on the Powell expeditions are as amusing today as on the day they were written:

> . . . tried to drink all the whiskey there was in town. The result was a falure [sic], as Jake Field persisted in making it faster than we could drink it.

> Jack Sumner, 1869

> . . . The present "City" [Green River] consisted of about thirteen houses, and some of these were of such complex construction that one hesitates whether to describe them as houses with canvas roofs, or tents with board sides.

> Frederick Dellenbaugh, 1871

The town started as a stage station and today ranks as the largest supplier of trona in the world. Trona is a rock that contains the raw material for soda ash, which is used in the production of everything from baking soda to laundry detergent and from glass to paper. An estimated 100 billion tons of trona rest below the surface surrounding Green River in deposits from an ancient landlocked lake. Ninety percent of domestic and 25 percent of global production of soda ash originates from Green River–area facilities.

The magnificent butte formations (called The Palisades) on the northern outskirts of Green River are the remains of prehistoric sea bottoms. The buttes named Castle Rock, Teapot

Dome, and Sugar Bowl have been made famous in a painting of Native Americans and trappers fording the Green River by nineteenth-century artist Thomas Moran, who also captured the beauty of Yellowstone.

The ◆ **Sweetwater County Historical Museum** has an excellent collection of Native American clothing and artifacts, informative displays on trona mining, a large collection of historic photographs of Green River, and extensive research materials on Sweetwater County. The museum is located on the ground floor of the County Courthouse at 80 West Flaming Gorge Way. Hours are from 9:00 A.M. to 5:00 P.M. on Monday through Friday year-round, and during July and August the museum is also open on Saturday from 1:00 to 5:00 P.M. For information call 872–6435 or 352–6715.

One historic Green River building you won't want to miss is the **Green River Brewery,** now occupied by a bar and lounge appropriately called The Brewery. Adam Braum built the first brewery in the Territory of Wyoming in 1872. It changed hands several times over the next several decades. In 1901 the new owner, Hugo Gaensslen, built a new brewery building from locally quarried stone and modeled it after the Chicago Water Tower, which has become a Windy City landmark. The brewery is on the National Register of Historic Places. It is located on West Railroad Street between North First West and Center Street.

You'll want to also visit the **Old Post Office** at 3 East Flaming Gorge Way. The brick Greek Revival building appears to be an unlikely place to chow down on some wonderful Mexican food, but take our word for it. **Rita's Fine Mexican Food** delivers what it promises. Prices for lunch and dinner are moderate. For information call 875–5503.

If you want to have a picnic and observe nature, journey down to **Scott's Bottom Nature Area.** You'll see a wide variety of plant species, from wild licorice to Russian olive, and wildlife abounds in this pristine oasis. A guidebook leads you on a half-mile loop trail. For information contact the Green River Parks and Recreation Department at 50 East Second Street or call 875–5000.

The fishing spots in southwestern Wyoming are part of the Green River drainage. To find cutthroat and lake trout and whitefish, go to the Green River Pioneer Trails. Head west on Interstate 80 to the LaBarge Road exit, then travel on Highway 372 for 10 miles and then east on County Road 60 to Pioneer Trails Park.

For more fishing information contact the Wyoming Fish and Game Department at 351 Astle Avenue, Green River 82935 or call 875–3223.

UINTA COUNTY

Fort Bridger ranks as one of Wyoming's longest continously set-tled sites. The first annual fur trapper rendezvous took place there in 1825, before the fort was constructed. In 1843 fur trapper and entrepreneur Jim Bridger built Fort Bridger with his partner Louis Vasquez. The Bridger–Vasquez partnership supplied emigrant wagon trains bound for Utah, Oregon, and California. The Mormon Church took over the property in 1855 after building its own Fort Supply in 1853. The Mormons burned Fort Bridger in 1857 after a skirmish with the federal government. Fort Bridger was rebuilt and used by the government until 1890.

The ◆ **Fort Bridger State Historic Site** re-creates the post and activities that went on there during the colorful pioneer days. The fort includes many original and reconstructed buildings, such as the Commanding Officer's Quarters (1884), Bridger & Vasquez Trading Post (1843), first schoolhouse in Wyoming (1860), Commissary Storehouse (1867), and Guardhouse (1887). The museum contains a wealth of information and displays on fur trappers, Native Americans, and the military. You'll also find weapons, uniforms, Native American artifacts, and personal belongings of Jim Bridger. The Fort Bridger State Historic Site is located several miles south of Interstate 80 on Business 80. Guided tours are available June 1 through September 30 for a small fee. Self-guided tours are free. For information call 782–3842.

On Labor Day weekend more than 50,000 modern-day mountain men and their families rendezvous at Fort Bridger for a reenactment of the past with authentic mountain man demonstrations, clothing, crafts, and encampment. View Native American dance contests, skilled knife-throwing, and muzzle-loader shoots the way they were practiced in the past.

Take the Piedmont Road exit from Interstate 80 to access the ghost town of Piedmont and the ◆ **Piedmont Kilns.** Back in 1869, Moses Byrne built five charcoal kilns north of Piedmont to provide charcoal to a smelter in Utah and for coke used by the Union Pacific for its steam engines. Three of the 30-foot by 30-

Charcoal kilns, Piedmont

foot kilns still stand, as do several buildings at the town site, which became deserted after the railroad moved the track farther north in 1901. Hard to imagine it now, but there were once fifteen hundred people living in Piedmont. Treasure seekers still scour the Piedmont area for gold that Butch Cassidy and his gang reportedly buried here. The beehive-shaped kilns are still well preserved.

Evanston is the last stop in this section of southern Wyoming. Check out **Pete's Ruck 'N Rye,** a funky old roadhouse located on the frontage road along Interstate 80; turn east after you take the Bear River Drive exit. It has a great jukebox and plenty of local flavor.

Like Rock Springs, Evanston grew as a railroad and mining town. Also like its neighbor to the east, Evanston suffered racial strife when Chinese miners were hired as strikebreakers in 1869 and a riot ensued, forcing the evacuation of Chinatown. In 1922 a fire destroyed a sacred Chinese temple, called a ◆ **Joss House,** that was built in 1870. A replica of the temple was completed in the early 1990s and stands on Depot Square, near Tenth and Front streets. It contains many artifacts salvaged from the 1922 fire. The original Joss House was one of only three in the United States when it was built. For information stop at the Chamber of Commerce Office, located in the 1906 Carnegie Library Building also in Depot Square at 36 Tenth Street, or call (800) 328–9708.

Conveniently, the Old Carnegie Library also houses the **Uinta County Historical Museum.** The museum has been in existence only since 1987, but it has done a good job of preserving the heritage of southwestern Wyoming. It includes fine collections of artifacts and memorabilia on Native American and Chinese history, as well as on ranching, the railroad, gambling, and bootlegging, which are all parts of Evanston's heritage. The museum is open 8:00 A.M. to 5:00 P.M. year-round and additionally from 10:00 A.M. to 4:00 P.M. on Saturday and Sunday during the summer. For information call 789–8745.

The 1901 Gothic **Depot** has an interesting history. After passenger train service stopped in 1983, the city acquired and restored the depot. When Amtrak revived passenger service through Wyoming in 1991, the depot's restored baggage room became the new passenger area. Evanston is also home to Wyoming's last remaining roundhouse. Ask at the chamber of commerce for directions.

From a geological standpoint, **The Overthrust Belt** near Evanston is part of a series of complex geological structures stretching from Alaska to Mexico that are rich in oil and gas deposits. The first major discovery near Evanston occurred in 1975 at the Pineview Field, 25 miles southwest of Evanston.

The **Bear River State Park** lies within the Evanston city limits. The park facilities are ideal for a day picnic, hiking, wildlife viewing, cycling, cross-country skiing, and other outdoor activities. Bear River State Park is located just south of exit 6, the Bear River Drive exit. The park headquarters telephone number is 789–6547.

Evanston features live pari-mutuel horse racing at **Wyoming Downs** 8 miles north on Highway 89. Thoroughbred and quarter horse racing takes place Memorial Day through Labor Day.

For quality Italian food try **Sorells'** at 125 Tenth Street. For restaurant hours and information call 789–8720. The **Pine Gables B&B** at 1049 Center Street was built in 1883 by Evanston's first merchant, A. V. Quinn. It operated as a European-style boardinghouse in the 1920s and 1930s. It takes its name from the structure's many gables and pine tree setting. Rates are in the $45 per night range for a double. Call 789–2069 for information and reservations.

CENTRAL WYOMING

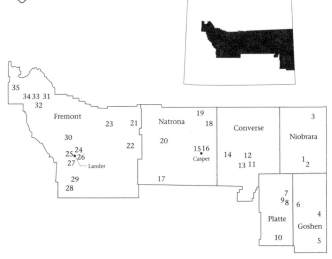

1. Stagecoach Museum
2. Redwood Water Tower
3. Sage and Cactus Village
4. Homesteader's Museum
5. Hawk Springs State Recreation Area
6. Fort Laramie National Historic Site
7. Hartville and Sunrise
8. Oregon Trail Ruts and Register Cliff
9. Guernsey State Park Museum
10. Diamond Guest Ranch, Inc.
11. Jackalope Capital of the World
12. Fort Fetterman
13. Ayres Natural Bridge
14. The Paisley Shawl/Hotel Higgins
15. Fort Caspar
16. Nicolaysen Art Museum and Discovery Center
17. Independence Rock
18. Teapot Rock
19. Midwest Museum
20. Hell's Half Acre
21. The Big Tipi
22. Castle Gardens
23. Yellowstone Drug Store
24. Sweetwater Grille
25. Piece of Cake Bed & Breakfast
26. Eagle Bronze, Inc. Foundry & Gallery
27. Sinks Canyon State Park
28. South Pass City State Historic Site
29. Atlantic City Mercantile
30. Sacajawea's Grave
31. Lazy L & B Ranch
32. Jakey's Fork Homestead
33. National Bighorn Sheep Interpretive Center
34. Old Yellowstone Garage
35. Tie Hack Monument

CENTRAL WYOMING

NIOBRARA COUNTY

Lusk (population 1,504) boomed with the onset of the gold rush in the Black Hills in the late 1800s and later with a post–World War II oil boom that eventually went bust after the wells dried up. The town lies at the intersection of Highway 20, which comes out of the east from Nebraska, and Highway 85, which virtually follows the Cheyenne-to-Deadwood/Black Hills stage line route. The stagecoach trip covered some 300 miles of rough roads and treacherous river crossings through Indian territory. What better location to situate the ◆ **Stagecoach Museum?**

The Stagecoach Museum occupies the former National Guard Armory at 322 S. Main Street. The transportation section houses more than stagecoaches. In addition, there's a fine collection of covered wagons, a dray wagon, Lusk's old street sprinkler, and early fire-fighting equipment. The centerpiece is a stagecoach used on the famed Cheyenne–Black Hills Stage and Express Line. Built by Abbott & Downing of Concord, New Hampshire, in the 1860s, the coach features a leather brace suspension system that eliminates the need for springs. A similar stagecoach is exhibited at the Smithsonian Institution in Washington, D.C.

You can explore four pioneer rooms, the front of the old iron-clad store moved in 1866 from the Silver Cliff townsite, an early doctor's office, and an ever-popular two-headed calf. The museum is open from 1:00 to 5:00 P.M. on Monday through Friday during May, June, September, and October. During July and August it's open from 1:00 to 8:00 P.M. on Tuesday through Saturday and from 2:00 to 8:00 P.M. on Sunday. For information call 334–3444.

Several miles east of town on Highway 20 you will find a restored ◆ **Redwood Water Tower,** one of few still standing in the country. The Fremont Elkhorn/Missouri Valley Railroad built the tower in 1886 to supply water for its steam engines. When the railroad tracks reached Lusk on July 13, 1886, a gold spike was driven with a silver hammer to commemorate the occasion. A little farther east you will locate a **Texas Trails Marker** honoring the cowboys who drove cattle from Texas to Montana between 1876 and 1897.

About 13 miles north of Lusk on Highway 18/85, there's a **Fort Hat Creek** interpretive sign marking the 1875 establishment of an outpost by soldiers from Fort Laramie. Ironically, the soldiers were disoriented and located the fort on Sage Creek in Wyoming instead of on Hat Creek in Nebraska. The **Hat Creek Monument** and the old fort site are located on private land a bit north and then 2 miles east on a county road and then southwest 1 mile on a gravel road. The marker and log building used as a stage station can easily be seen from the road. Please respect the rights of the property owner.

Hat Creek played a prominent role in the surrender of Chief Crazy Horse. The brave Sioux chief sent a messenger to Hat Creek on May 1, 1877, announcing his intention to surrender. The message was then telegraphed to Camp Robinson. On May 6 Chief Crazy Horse rode to Red Cloud Agency, shook hands with General Crook's emissary, and smoked the peace pipe, concluding the Great Sioux War.

For a truly Western experience drive 50 miles north of Lusk on Highway 85 and then 2½ miles north of Mule Creek Junction to the ❖ **Sage and Cactus Village.** You get to sleep in a tipi bed and breakfast on bluffs overlooking the Cheyenne River. You'll wake up to coffee brewing over a campfire and a hearty breakfast. The Sage and Cactus Village is open daily Memorial Day to Labor Day (earlier or later, weather permitting). Rates run $40 for two people per night. For information and reservations call 663–7653.

A real Western character, **Mother Featherlegs Shepard,** earned her name and reputation. She used to ride herd on her cattle with her red pantaloons fluttering in the breeze like a feather. The roadhouse madam on the Cheyenne–Black Hills Stage Line was murdered by Dangerous Dick Davis in 1879 over $1,500. A monument to Mother Featherlegs is located 10 miles southwest of Lusk. Access to the site is via a dirt road just south of the rest area on Highway 85.

Two architecturally interesting buildings in Lusk are the 1919 **Niobrara County Courthouse** and the 1919 Renaissance/Italianate **Niobrara County Library**, the last Carnegie library in Wyoming still used as a library. Both buildings are under consideration for inclusion on the National Register of Historic Places.

The library is located at 425 South Main Street. The dilapidated **Yellow Hotel** south of the Chicago Northwestern Railroad Depot saw much better days when owner Madame Del Burke ran a very successful brothel at the hotel. Lusk owes its water and electrical systems to her generosity. She reportedly owned many of the city bonds for those services.

The **Legend of Rawhide** takes place in early July each year. Unlike many homegrown productions, this pageant of the Wyoming West has been perfected over the nearly half a century it has been produced by the citizens of Lusk. Festivities include two live performances with a cast of two hundred, country-and-western concert and barbecue, an art show, parade, and outdoor pancake breakfasts. For information and dates call (800) 223–LUSK.

GOSHEN COUNTY

Goshen County serves as the jumping-off point of the Oregon, Mormon, and California Trails in Wyoming. The first major stopping area was at Fort Laramie. The fort also was an important stop on the Pony Express route and the Cheyenne–Black Hills Stage Line. But before we head for Fort Laramie we'll first make a stop at Torrington on Highway 85, about 57 miles southeast of Lusk and only 8 miles from the Nebraska border.

The ◆ **Homesteader's Museum** features the Cheyenne–Black Hills Stagecoach made famous in Buffalo Bill's Wild West Show after the turn of the century. The museum is located in the 1926 Union Pacific Depot just south of town and across from Torrington's largest employer, the Holly Sugar factory. The depot is a pleasantly ornate structure designed by the noted architectural firm of Gilbert Stanley Underwood. Inside, you will find materials from the well-known 4A Ranch, historic photographs of the area, and information and artifacts relating to Wyoming's homesteaders. The museum is open 10:00 A.M. to 5:00 P.M. Monday through Saturday and 1:00 to 4:00 P.M. on Sunday during the summer. Call 532–3879 for information and winter hours.

Twenty-two miles south of Torrington just off Highway 85, you'll find a pleasant park that is truly off the beaten path. ◆ **Hawk Springs State Recreation Area** provides excellent fishing and picnic facilities, but the real draw is the presence of a blue heron rookery on the site. With a little patience you can see blue herons, great horned owls, wood ducks, a variety of teal, and other birds. Be sure to bring along a pair of binoculars. Fees are minimal, a few dollars per vehicle per night. For information contact the Hawk Springs State Recreational Area at 836–2334.

Traveling west on Highway 26 you come to the town of Lingle, within 2 miles of the August 19, 1854, **Grattan Massacre Site,** the first major confrontation between United States soldiers and Native Americans. The incident was touched off when Lt. John Grattan went to a Sioux village to arrest a tribal member for killing a steer. A shot was fired, panic ensued, and Grattan and his twenty-eight-man force were killed. The massacre led to the Plains Indian Wars and the eventual removal of tribes to reservations in the late 1800s.

❖ **Fort Laramie National Historic Site** is a premier reconstruction and provides excellent interpretive programs and fort tours. Although Fort Laramie is open year-round, the place really steps back in time during the summer, when park rangers dress in period clothes and become the characters that made Fort Laramie a vibrant part of the Wyoming West from 1841 to the end of the Indian Wars in 1890. Earlier, in 1834, William Sublette had erected a trading post at a nearby site. Sublette sold his Fort William in 1836 to the American Fur Company, which later rebuilt it a mile up the Laramie River at the site of present Fort Laramie. The government purchased the fort in 1841.

Without a doubt, Fort Laramie is a must-stop for today's travelers, as it was for those travelers during the past century and before. It was a gathering spot for Native Americans, trappers, traders, gold seekers, Pony Express riders, and emigrants. By the time emigrants reached Fort Laramie, they had already journeyed 650 miles on the Oregon Trail from Independence, Missouri, and still had some 1200 more miles stretching out into the desert and mountain country before them. Six-mule wagon teams were the preferred method of travel, but oxen were often substituted for mules because they were less expensive. A six-mule team commanded $600, while eight oxen could be purchased for $200. Emigrants spent between $800 to $1,200 to properly outfit themselves for the journey.

Fort Laramie

There were many dangers, as one emigrant recorded:

We passed Fort Laramie yesterday and obtained several little articles needed in camp. At this camp, an emigrant, who, with his wife, was travelling with another family, murdered the other man and his wife. He then took possession of the man's team and provisions and he and his wife started the return trip to the Missouri River, reporting that they had become discouraged and would go no further. Within a day, the dead bodies of the murdered couple were discovered and the officers at Fort Laramie notified. We heard that they were apprehended, tried at Fort Laramie at the charge of murder, convicted and hanged. We did not learn their names . . .

Old Bedlam, within the fort near the west end of the parade grounds, is the oldest remaining structure in Wyoming, having been built in 1849. Through the years it served as post headquarters, officers' quarters, and living quarters for other post residents. Additional original structures worthy of a tour include the bakery, cavalry barracks, commissary, guardhouse, officers' houses, powder magazine, and surgeon's quarters. There's plenty of history to be learned at Fort Laramie, and there are rumors of a ghost or two inhabiting the buildings. Ask your guide for details. The visitors center is open from 8:00 A.M. to 4:30 P.M. every day except federal holidays between October and April. There are extended hours from mid-May to late September. The fort grounds are open till dusk every day of the year. The Fort Laramie National Historic Site is located 3 miles southwest of the town of Fort Laramie off Highway 26. For information call 837–2221.

PLATTE COUNTY

Following Highway 26 west into Platte County, you'll cross the North Platte River at Guernsey (population 1,155). But first take a pleasant diversion to the virtual ghost towns of ◆ **Hartville** (population 78) and ◆ **Sunrise** (population, you guess) by turning north on Highway 270 about 1 mile east of Guernsey. The countryside will turn into a series of red gorges, rolling rangeland, and pine- and juniper-covered hills. Four miles north sits picturesque Hartville, Wyoming's oldest incorporated town still in existence. Prospectors looking for gold, silver, copper, and other minerals in the Eureka Canyon area settled Hartville in the 1870s. The town dates from 1884 and was incorporated in 1900, when it was a thriving city with a population of 750 and an opera house. After the copper deposit played out in the late 1880s, an iron deposit discovered near Sunrise kept the town going. The Hartville Uplift contains one of Wyoming's richest mineral deposits.

Stop in at the **Old Miners' Bar,** the state's oldest recreation area, for a look at one of the most interesting back bars in Wyoming. It was crafted in Germany in 1864 and traveled the final miles of its journey to Hartville by wagon in 1881. The old stone buildings (especially the town jail) and shops with their false fronts provide a great backdrop for photos. Ask the locals for directions to boothill (that's the cemetery, for you non-Westerners).

You can always discover some interesting sights there. The last gunfight took place on Main Street in 1912.

With a large Italian population, it's not surprising that the **Venice Bar** serves excellent Italian dinners. You must make reservations, however. Prices are moderate. For restaurant hours, information, and reservations, call 836–2881.

Sunrise, 1 mile east of Hartville on Highway 318, possesses its own attraction. The Colorado Fuel and Iron Corporation employed some seven hundred workers at its Chicago Mine, known as Glory Hole. In 1942 it produced a million tons of ore. One of the nation's largest open-pit iron ore mines, it has been idle since 1980. Still, you can get an understanding of the scope of the mining activity that went on for decades. A few brick houses and the YMCA still remain.

The Guernsey area offers a lot for history and sports buffs alike. For those following the Oregon Trail, take a short jaunt to see two famous landmarks, the ❖ **Oregon Trail Ruts** and ❖ **Register Cliff.** The combined effect of the large number of wagons traversing the Oregon Trail and the relatively soft sandstone outcroppings resulted in wagon wheel ruts 2 to 6 feet deep, a visible connection with one of the largest non-forced migrations of people in the world. Heavy oxen hooves and hundreds of thousands of wheels ground away the sandstone above the banks of the North Platte River. As you step into the ruts, you feel the pull of history. It's hard not to be in awe of stamina of the everyday people who traveled thousands of miles across this harsh land for a better life. The ruts and interpretive signs are located half a mile southeast of Guernsey, off Highway 26. Follow the signs.

Emigrants carved their names into Register Cliff, located two miles southeast of Guernsey. The earliest names date back to 1829. For information on both the Oregon Trail Ruts and Register Cliff contact Wyoming State Parks & Cultural Resources in Cheyenne at 777–6323.

Guernsey was named after Charles Guernsey, an area rancher, legislator, and early promoter of the Guernsey Dam and Reservoir. He also wrote *Wyoming Cowboy Days*. **Guernsey State Park** provides ample recreational opportunities and camping facilities. The high bluffs and warm waters are a favorite with day-trippers and overnight campers. The park features a 6.2-mile **Volksmarch** along a scenic trail at an elevation of 4,500 feet,

Oregon Trail ruts near Guernsey

overlooking the dam, reservoir, and downstream countryside. The trail is rated a difficulty of four on a five-point scale and is one of the most demanding in Wyoming's State Park system. The park has more than 6,200 acres of land and nearly 2,400 ares of water. It encompasses 142 campsites, three day-use areas and thirty-seven cabin sites. For park and campsite information call 836–2334.

In the 1930s the Civilian Conservation Corps (CCC) constructed a series of rock and log structures throughout the park and much of the park's road system. One section of the park road is affectionately called "Mae West Drive" because of its beautiful curves.

One of the most impressive rock buildings built by the CCC contains the ◆ **Guernsey State Park Museum.** Its large arched rock entrance, native flagstone floors, hand-hewn roof timbers, and wrought-iron fixtures reflect quality craftsmanship. The exhibits, also created in the 1930s, relate how people adaptated to the Guernsey environment through the ages. Museum hours are 10:00 A.M. to 6:00 P.M. seven days a week from May through Labor Day. For information call 836–2900.

For a pleasant drive, weather and time of year permitting, take the paved road marked Greyrocks Road or Power Plant Road (beginning as Highway 109 South and ending up as Highway 67) before arriving in Wheatland. It passes through some interesting country and will take you by the Greyrocks Reservoir.

For a restful place to spend the evening, make reservations at **The Blackbird Inn** in Wheatland (population 3,271). The 1910 Victorian B&B, operated by Dan Brecht, displays antique furnishings. Each room suggests a theme, from "Alaska" and "Whale" to "Wyoming" and "LaRamie." You'll enjoy the front porch with its swing and wicker furniture as the brilliant Wyoming sunset unfolds before you. Overnight rates are in the under $50 to $75 range. For reservations call 322–4540.

The area around the town of Chugwater (population 192) has some interesting history and a great place to stay. The Swan Land and Cattle Company called Chugwater its headquarters although most of its stockholders called Scotland home. It was the most famous and last of the great ranch spreads still in existence in the 1880s. At one time more than 113,000 head of cattle grazed on its land. The brutal 1886–87 winter killed off many of the ranch's cattle, but the company reorganized and avoided going out of business for another fifty years. After the turn of the century, however, the famous cattle company switched to raising sheep.

According to legend, the name Chugwater came from the sound stampeding buffalo made as they hit the water after being driven off the bluffs by Native Americans. Chugwater is home to another famous ranch, the ◆ **Diamond Guest Ranch, Inc.,** where weary travelers can spend a day or week and experience ranch life. The ranch was founded by Thoroughbred horse breeder George R. Rainsford in 1880. Four generations later, it continues as a working ranch with many of the original buildings in use. Here you can go on a trail ride, angle for fish from under a cottonwood tree, or just plain relax . . . the Diamond Guest Ranch has it all, plus good food. Other activities and facilities include a Saturday night dance, hayrides, a swimming pool, breakfast on the trail, horseshoes, and a steak house. The Diamond Guest Ranch is open from May 15 to October 15. You can book a deluxe or ranch room (in the historic 1878 ranch house) or camp at one of the many campsites with or without water and electrical hookups. Room rates start at $46 per night. The ranch is located 14 miles west of Chugwater on Diamond Road. For more information and reservations call 422–3567 or (800) 932–4222.

The Diamond Guest Ranch is also home to the annual **Chugwater Chili Cook-off** held in mid-May. It's the largest single-day event in the whole state and a great family affair. Events include a dance, trail rides, and a giant outdoor barbecue. For information call 422–3345.

On the way out of town, stop on Main Street and treat yourself at the **Chugwater Soda Fountain,** one of the oldest soda fountains in Wyoming and the maker of some great ice-cream treats.

Unfortunately, it's time to get on Interstate 25 for a while. Head north for the last stop in Platte County, Glendo, which sits alongside the original site of the 1861 Horseshoe Stage Station of the Hockaday-Ligget Stage Line. John "Portugee" Phillips stopped at the station in 1866 during his famous ride to Fort Laramie in blizzard conditions to seek help for Fort Phil Kearny after the late-December Fetterman Massacre. Another colorful western figure, Buffalo Bill Cody, rode for the Pony Express out of the Horseshoe Stage Station.

The major attraction at Glendo today is the **Glendo State Park,** with 12,500 acres of unbelievably clear reservoir waters for fishing, waterskiing, sailing, and power boating. From your pine-forested campsite you can view beautiful 10,272-foot Laramie Peak in the Medicine Bow National Forest to the southwest. A small buffalo herd grazes near the south side of the reservoir. Entrance fees are several dollars per vehicle. For park and campsite information call 735–4433.

CONVERSE COUNTY

There's no con in Converse County unless, of course, you consider the jackalope. Long a source of speculation and heated arguments, the infamous jackalope calls Converse County home. In fact, Douglas is the ◆ **Jackalope Capital of the World,** as evidenced by the giant statue of a jackalope in the middle of town at Jackalope Square. Obviously Douglas stands a hare above other would-be contenders for the honor.

Scientifically known as *pegirus lepuslopus ineptus,* the jackalope's lightning-like speed is partly to blame for the legions of doubters. But, for clear evidence of their existence, one only has to look at the large ruts in the earthscape just south of Douglas to see where ancient predecessors of today's jackalopes, the dynalopes and jackaoaurs, roamed.

The **Wyoming Pioneer Memorial Museum** on the Wyoming State Fairgrounds in Douglas has an especially good saddle collection. Also on display are the original bar (crafted by Brunswick in England in 1914) from the LaBonte Inn, guns and memorabilia from the famous Johnson County War, Native American clothing and decorative arts, and a collection of Western art. The museum is open year-round. For information call 358–9288.

Thirty-two miles south of Douglas on Highway 94 you'll stumble on Esterbrook, a copper-mining town established in 1886 but soon relegated to the forgotten past. The main attraction is a rustic log church, **Esterbrook Chapel,** still used for numerous weddings, under the beauty of nearby Laramie Peak.

Take Highway 93 for 11 miles northwest out of Douglas to reach ◆ **Fort Fetterman,** named after Lt. Col. William J. Fetterman, who was killed by Native Americans in 1866 at what became known as the Fetterman Massacre near Fort Kearny. Fort Fetterman was built in 1867 as a supply station to troops engaged in subduing Indian uprisings.

Major Dye, who was assigned to build the fort, wrote that the post was "situated on a plateau . . . above the valley of the Platte, being neither so low as to be seriously affected by the rains or snow; nor so high and unprotected as to suffer from the winter winds."

Needless to say, Dye underestimated the Wyoming winds and winter. Hard toil and brutal winter storms earned the fort the reputation as a hardship post by men stationed there. After the Treaty of 1868, Forts Reno, Phil Kearny and C. F. Smith were abandoned, leaving Fort Fetterman as the lone army outpost near the disputed Indian territory. The fort was abandoned in 1882 after the Native Americans were moved to reservations and no longer posed a threat.

The restored Officer's Quarters houses a museum of the fort's history. Living-history programs are presented during the summer season, which runs from Memorial Day through Labor Day. Visitors center hours are from 9:00 A.M. to 5:00 P.M. daily. The grounds are open from sunrise to sunset. Fort Fetterman Days is held in early July with artillery, infantry, and cavalry demonstrations as well as crafts, folklore, and frontier music. For information call 358–2864 or 777–7014.

We hesitate to tell you about ◆ **Ayres Natural Bridge** for fear it will become overrun by tourists. As it is now, few people besides the "in the know" locals find their way to this peaceful sanctuary. The cascading waters of LaPrele Creek flow under the 150-foot span formed by nature through the centuries. The sound of the flowing water virtually mesmerizes you. This is truly one of Wyoming's unspoiled treasures. It's no wonder that emigrants found Ayres Natural Bridge so refreshing. One emigrant wrote about stopping here:

> Today we camped near the natural bridge and laid by to wash and rest our cattle. We noticed it had become general for the stock to begin to suffer and lag with the increasing roughness of the country. It is more noticeable among the horses than with the cattle. We saw several bands of buffalo today but got no meat. Grass is scarce and seems to be getting more and more scarce the further we go, having been used up by those ahead of us . . .

It all started more than 280,000,000 years ago. The Casper Sandstone Formation was laid down during the Pennsylvanian Age. During the ensuing eons, water from the Laramie Range gradually eroded away the soft sandstone base, leaving a natural bridge 50 feet high. While other natural bridges exist around the world, Ayres Natural Bridge is one of the few with water still flowing underneath.

Adding to the beauty, Ayres Natural Bridge is framed by sheer red sandstone walls, giving an amphitheater effect. Elm and cottonwood shade trees provide a picturesque setting for a relaxed afternoon or evening.

Pioneer travelers to the bridge included Robert Stuart in 1812 and Captain B. L. E. Bonneville in 1832. A number of emigrants have left their mark, carving their names or initials into the red sandstone cliff walls. Early trappers and prospectors plied the lower LaPrele Creek area for fur and gold. By 1851, Mormons who traversed the nearby Oregon and California trails established abundant gardens in the valley with the help of irrigation ditches. Large storehouses preserved surpluses to be shared with other Mormons moving westward to Utah.

Not all area inhabitants found the natural bridge inviting. Ancient Native American legends tell of an evil spirit, King of Beasts, who was thought to live beneath the bridge. According to legend, a hunting party sought shelter under the arch of the bridge during a terrifying lightning- and thunderstorm. A lightning bolt struck and killed one of the braves. The others fled in terror, later telling their chief how the hills opened up and the King of Beasts emerged with long, dagger-like teeth and flashing eyes to swallow the life of the young brave.

In 1881 Alva Ayres, an early freighter and bullwhacker, purchased the property and used it as headquarters for his shipping business. Two years after his death in 1918, his heirs donated the bridge and fifteen acres of land to Converse County for designation as Ayres Natural Bridge.

To reach this retreat, follow Interstate 25 for 11 miles northwest of Douglas to exit 151. The bridge is located 4 miles south at the end of County Road 13. The park is open April 1 through October 31 from 8:00 A.M. to 8:00 P.M. Overnight camping, not to exceed three consecutive nights, is permitted with written permission of the caretaker. For information call 358–3532.

With your arrival at Glenrock (population 2,153), about 21 miles northwest of Douglas, you are in oil country as evidenced by the pumpers on the outskirts of town. Oil was first discovered around 1916, whereupon the town swelled to more than five thousand people. A second major strike in 1949 brought another round of prosperity. Today, the town's economic viability comes from another energy source, the Dave Johnston Power Plant, 6 miles east of town.

The name Glenrock referred to the large rock in the glen at the edge of the townsite. Kit Carson guided John C. Fremont's first expedition of the West to this site in 1842. Names of a number of the estimated 350,000 emigrants who passed here carved their names and dates into the **Rock in the Glen.** It is located in the park on the south side of Highway 20/87 at the west end of Glenrock.

The **Deer Creek Station** was built in the 1850s and served as an important stop on the Overland Stage, Pony Express, and wagon trail routes. Native Americans torched it in 1866. A historical Deer Creek Station marker is located at Fourth and Cedar Streets in Glenrock.

A narrow gorge a few miles west of present-day Casper forced emigrants traveling on the south bank of the North Platte River to cross over to the other side. The sheer numbers of people and wagons necessitated a several-day wait to be ferried safely across the river. Some of the more impatient tried to swim across and drowned.

An entrepreneur named John Richard (pronounced "Reshaw"), along with four other French traders, built the first bridge to span the North Platte River, just above the mouth of Deer Creek, northwest of Glenrock. Richard and his partners expected huge profits, but their dreams were washed down the river, along with the wooden toll bridge, during the spring flood of 1852.

Even some Wyomingites don't know about ◆ **The Paisley Shawl/Hotel Higgins** located at 416 West Birch Street in Glenrock. Reopened in 1980 after fifty years, the restaurant elegantly serves a select and scrumptious menu of four choices, such as ribs, shrimp scampi, chicken Dijon, and New York pepper steak. You can order the full meal with an appetizer, salad, soup, and dessert included, or choose a la carte. Prices are moderate to expensive but every bit worth it. The restaurant's name comes from a circa 1865 family heirloom shawl made in Paisley, Scotland. Hours are generally Monday through Saturday 11:30 A.M. to 1:30 P.M. and 6:00 to 9:30 P.M. Call 436–9212 for seasonal hour changes.

Hotel Higgins was built in 1916 and claimed to be the "Finest Hotel North of Denver." It is listed on the National Register of Historic Places. The original terrazzo tile remains throughout the hotel. In its early days the hotel hosted William Jennings Bryan and Governor Robert Carey. The current owners, Jack and Margaret Doll, restored the rooms to their 1900 appearance, and Hotel Higgins now operates as a bed-and-breakfast inn serving a champagne breakfast in the enclosed porch area. Each room is decorated differently and furnished with a brass, iron, or carved-wood bed. Adjoining rooms are available for families. Rates are $58 for a double and $68 for a suite. For hotel and restaurant information or reservations call 436–9212.

NATRONA COUNTY

Take the Old Glenrock Highway (Highway 20/26) west out of Glenrock to avoid the hassle of Interstate 80 and enter the **Edness Kimball Wilkins State Park** just east of Hat Six Road. Situated alongside the North Platte River, the park's 315 acres filled with cottonwoods provide a shady oasis for an afternoon picnic. Walk along the tree-lined trails or wade in the swimming pond to cool off from the summer heat. Bring your binoculars; there's an abundance of birds and wildlife to observe along the North Platte.

Good populations of rainbow, brown, and cutthroat trout and channel catfish can be found here also. For more information on fishing in the Platt/Powder drainages, contact Wyoming Game and Fish at 2800 Pheasant Drive, Casper 82604 or call 234-9185.

Continuing on Highway 20/26 you arrive at Wyoming's oil capital, Casper. The city grew up along the banks of the North Platte River at the convergence of all major westward trails. Turn south on Wyoming Boulevard and proceed to ◆ **Fort Caspar** at 4001 Fort Caspar Road. Originally started as a trading post in 1859, a volunteer cavalry company guarded the bridge and Platte Bridge Station beginning in 1861. On July 26, 1865, Lt. Caspar Collins and a small detachment, sent to escort a military wagon train, were attacked while crossing the bridge. Collins and four of his twenty men were killed. The three-wagon military train that Caspar's detachment was sent to protect was also attacked and destroyed by a band of Arapahoe, Cheyenne, and Sioux Indians. After four hours of conflict, twenty-two soldiers lay dead at the Battle of Red Buttes. There's a **Red Buttes Battle Marker** located on the north side of Highway 220 at a paved turnout about ½ mile west of Robertson Road. In tribute to Caspar, the government officially changed the post's name from Platte Bridge Station to Fort Caspar (a Fort Collins already existed in Colorado). Two years later the government abandoned the fort.

In 1936 the Works Progress Administration (WPA) reconstructed a number of the log buildings using sketches made by Caspar Collins in 1863. An interpretive center/museum opened in 1983. The fort buildings are open mid-May through mid-September from 9:00 A.M. to 6:00 P.M. Monday through Friday,

9:00 A.M. to 5:00 P.M. on Saturday, and noon to 5:00 P.M. on Sunday. In addition, the interpretive center is open during the winter from 9:00 A.M. to 5:00 P.M. Monday through Friday and 1:00 to 4:00 P.M. on Sunday. For information call 235–8462.

Casper was incorporated in 1889 and the nearly simultaneous discovery of oil assured its growth and a series of economic booms and busts tied to the energy industry. Many of downtown Casper's buildings are the result of the 1920s oil boom, and a walking tour of Casper is an interesting way to spend a few hours. You can pick up a **Self-Guided Walking Tour** brochure from the Casper Historic Preservation Commission at Fort Caspar or at the Casper Area Chamber of Commerce office at 500 North Center Street. Check out the following unique structures. The 1940 **Courthouse** at 200 N. Center Street, built by the WPA, features an intricate frieze depicting the heritage of Casper. The 1921 **Rialto Theater** at 102 E. Second Street has decorative cornices and a great marquee. Incidentally, you can attend any show at the Rialto for only $1.75.

At 302 South David Street you'll find a late–Gothic Revival **fire station** with CASPER FIRE STATION 1 spelled out on the frieze above the fire truck entrances. The terra-cotta shield at the top of the building lists 1921 as the construction date. The fire station was added to the National Register of Historic Places in November 1993. Mission/Spanish and Colonial Revival architectural styles combine to create an interesting structure at **230 West Yellowstone** which housed the Casper Auto Company from 1918 until 1970. A red-tiled roof cornice and white terra-cotta detailing give it a distinctive look. It garnered a spot on the National Register of Historic Places in February 1994. There are many other interesting Casper buildings, but we'll let you discover them on your own. While you are still in the downtown area go look at the statue of **Prometheus,** the Titan who stole fire from Olympus and gave it to man, in front of the Natrona County Library at 307 E. Second Street.

Two blocks away at 400 East Collins Drive, is the intriguing ❖ **Nicolaysen Art Museum and Discovery Center.** The Nic is a great place to browse, view special exhibits, purchase unique art items from regional artists in the gift shop, and bring the kids for a fun-filled day. It celebrates art with invitational shows and special events. It provides kids of all ages a hands-on creative experience with a variety of activities in the Discovery Center. The art museum is open Tuesday through Sunday from 10:00 A.M. to 5:00 P.M. and on Thursday until 8:00 P.M. There is a $2.00 admission fee for adults and $1.00 for children, but on the first and third Thursdays of each month admittance is free. One final comment: The structure containing the Nicolaysen Art Museum and Discovery Center is the beautifully refurbished Old Casper Lumber Company building. For information on the exhibit schedule and other items call 235–5247.

For a funky experience stop in at **Dr. Spokes Cyclery & Bicycles & Pedal Car Museum** at 240 South Center Street. It's open in the summer 9:00 A.M. to 8:00 P.M. weekdays and on weekends from 9:00 A.M. to 5:00 P.M. For information call 265–7740.

At the Natrona County Airport you'll find the **Casper Centennial Mural**. In this 9½-by-28½-foot oil painting, artist Richard Jacobi has worked a variety of images from Casper history into a rich tapestry. The mural includes twenty-eight different scenes and is one of the largest paintings in the country done on a single piece of canvas.

Two side trips out of Casper are worthy of attention. First take Highway 220 southwest about 10 miles out of Casper to the **Goose Egg Inn.** Locals regularly dine here for steaks and other specialties. Appropriately, the address is 10580 Goose Egg Road. For hours and reservation information call 473–8838.

The nearby area is loaded with history. Spreading out along the North Platte River, Wyoming's largest and most famous ranch, **The Goose Egg Ranch,** served as a setting for Owen Wister's *The Virginian*. It was founded by the Searight Brothers from Texas and subsequently owned by generations of Governor Carey's family, and was later renamed the CY Ranch. A portion of the ranch land was plotted as part of Casper. The original 1877 ranch house was torn down in the early 1950s.

From the Goose Egg Ranch it's time to make tracks for ◆ **Independence Rock** 42 miles southwest from Casper on Highway 220. The best known of all of the Oregon Trail landmarks, and the most poignant, is called the "Register of the Desert." The 190-foot-high granite outcropping contains an estimated fifty thousand names inscribed by wagon train emigrants.

It earned its name when explorer William Sublette celebrated the Fourth of July at the rock in 1830. He wrote,

> Most of our company visited the summit of Independence Rock, which was reached with much difficulty but without accident. We found the rock literally covered with the names of emigrants. Some of these names were written with chalk, some were cut with a cold chisel, whilst ohters [sic] were written with tar . . .

Near Independence Rock, Ella Watson, also known as Cattle Kate, scored another first for Wyoming women, having the dubious honor of being the first woman hanged in Wyoming. Ella and bar owner Jim Averill had the annoying habit of putting their brand on other people's cattle until they were finally strung up for their misdeeds by their neighbors.

The second excursion from Casper before continuing westward involves taking Interstate 25 north 21 miles and then Highway 259 north for 4½ miles near Teapot Creek. On the right-hand (east) side of the road, you will see the remnants of the landmark whose name is associated with one of the biggest political scandals to come out of Washington.

◆ **Teapot Rock** (don't look for a teapot anymore—two tornadoes in the 1920s destroyed the handle and spout) is clearly visible from the dirt turnout. The Teapot Rock is located on private property, so don't trespass for a better look. The Teapot Dome scandal erupted when President Harding's Secretary of the Interior, Albert Fall, leased the Teapot Dome oil fields to Mammoth Oil Company (owned by Harry F. Sinclair) without proper bidding. Wyoming senator John Kendrick called for a complete investigation in 1922, and after a six-year investigation Fall was finally convicted of accepting a $100,000 bribe and spent a year in federal prison.

Continuing on, you'll pass the famous Salt Creek Oilfields, one of Wyoming's largest and still pumping after all these years. Then you'll arrive at Midwest (population 495). Proceed to the Town Hall at 531 Peake Street and inquire about the ◆ **Midwest Museum.** If the museum's not open, they'll give you the key and tell you to lock up when you are finished. It's a delightful and informative little museum that presents the history of the town, nearby ghost towns, and the Salt Creek Oilfields. You'll learn that the first claim was issued in 1883, oil was first discovered in 1889, and the first oil well drilled in 1908 at a depth of 1,050 feet. The area's population peaked at around 9,500 people in 1929; the company-owned hotel was capable of feeding 1,200 people per hour. To contact the Midwest Town Hall call 437–6513.

You might consider one final excursion out of Casper. **Historic Trails Expeditions** offers a number of trail rides via horseback or a Conestoga wagon, or you can float down the North Platte River on a raft. The tours range from several hours to several days. Meals and sleeping equipment are provided. You can follow the Oregon Trail or Pony Express Routes or track down the whereabouts of Butch Cassidy and that Hole in the Wall Gang. For expedition information and reservations, call 266-4868.

About 42 miles west of Casper on Highway 20/26 you leave the earth and look out across ◆ **Hell's Half Acre.** It's a wonderful spot for some photo ops of some of the more unusual Wyoming badlands. Here, Indians drove herds of buffalo off the cliffs to their deaths in order to obtain food and clothing. Captain Bonneville's expedition stopped here in 1833. There's even a Hell's Half Acre Post Office and a restaurant/store where you can pick up a postcard or two.

FREMONT COUNTY

If you're running short of cash and are in the mood to do a bit of prospecting, then a trip to the Lost Cabin area near Lysite is in the offing. Turn north at Moneta (population 10) on to Highway 176 (Lysite-Moneta Road). The pavement stops about 8 miles later at Lysite, where you might want to quench your thirst and inquire about road conditions at the country store before venturing on to Lost Cabin, 3 miles east.

As the story goes, prospectors extracted thousands of dollars of gold from a rich lode before Indians attacked and killed all but one or two of the miners, who escaped to the nearest town. Despite repeated attempts, the Lost Cabin and Lost Cabin Mine were never rediscovered. The Lost Cabin site is home to ◆ **The Big Tipi,** as Native Americans named the mansion built by Wyoming sheep millionaire John B. Odie in 1900. Odie outfitted the mansion with elaborately carved fireplace mantles, expensive chandeliers, Oriental rugs, and intricate stained glass. The mansion features an unusual octagonal tower. Outside, Odie constructed a greenhouse, dance hall, and aviary to house his collection of exotic birds. The mansion is located on private property, but it can be viewed discreetly from the road.

Back at Moneta, this time take Garden City Road 459 for 21 miles south and then BLM Road 2107 east to ◆ **Castle Gardens,** a premier archaeological site with ancient rock carvings. This is the largest and finest collection of petroglyphs in Wyoming. Perhaps the most famous is the Great Turtle petroglyph which disappeared from Castle Gardens for many years only to mysteriously reappear years later at the Wyoming State Museum. It is periodically displayed at the museum in Cheyenne. Another mystery surrounding the Great Turtle is why a snapping water turtle from the Mississippi or Missouri Rivers would appear in a petroglyph in arid Wyoming. Inquire about road conditions before attempting this journey, but it is well worth the effort and bumpy roads.

After a few hours of exploring in Castle Gardens and driving the 21 miles of semiarid country between Moneta and Shoshoni (population 497), you'll be ready for a milk shake or malt at the ◆ **Yellowstone Drug Store** at 127 Main Street. Over a season, the Yellowstone churns some thirty-five thousand rich milk shakes for travelers. You can also order hamburgers and other fare. Prices are inexpensive. It is hard to picture now, but during Shoshoni's boom years the town supported twenty-three saloons, two banks, two mercantile establishments, and several livery and feed stables. Head south one block from the drugstore and take a right before the railroad tracks for a look at a jail more than one hundred years old. Imagine how it felt to spend the hot desert summers or frigid Wyoming winters behind those bars.

Boysen State Park stretches from the outskirts of Shoshoni into the Wind River Canyon, a spectacular drive we'll pick up when we travel to Thermopolis in the Northern Wyoming section later in this book. The first white men in the area were with the Ashley Fur Party in 1825. The original dam was built in 1908 by Asmus Boysen, for whom the reservoir and park are named. The CB&Q Railroad laid tracks through the Wind River Canyon in 1911 and ended up suing Boysen after the tracks were flooded because of the dam. They won the suit and had Boysen's dam

Petroglyphs, Castle Gardens

dynamited. The existing dam was constructed in 1951 and Boysen became a state park in 1956. There are plenty of both day-use and overnight facilities on the 76 miles of shoreline. For information call 876-2796.

Twenty-two miles southwest of Shoshoni on Highway 26/789 is Riverton, the home of the mid-October **Cowboy Poets Roundup** featuring the best poets and performers in the region, who serve up their poems and music. The event takes place at Central Wyoming College and tickets are less than $10 per person. For information call the Riverton Chamber of Commerce at (800) 325–2732.

Hudson (population 392), another 14 miles southwest, claims two fine restaurants. **Svilar's Bar & Dining Room,** at 173

South Main Street, specializes in melt-in-your-mouth steaks. Duncan Hines once visited the restaurant and called it one of the best places he had ever eaten at. For information or reservations call 332–4516. Across the street, the **Club El Toro,** at 132 South Main Street, also features fine beef. Call 332–4627. Prices at both eating establishments are moderate.

The Fremont County Pioneer Museum, at 630 Lincoln Street in Lander, includes an eclectic collection of pioneer items both inside and outside. You'll see a 1929 Model A, wooden coal wagon, antique printing press, re-created general store, and pioneer parlor and kitchen. The log cabin reached from the side door of the main museum is the original museum, built in 1935. The museum is open 10:00 A.M. to 5:00 P.M. Monday through Friday and 1:00 to 4:00 P.M. on Saturday from June 1 through mid-September. The rest of the year, hours are 1:00 to 5:00 P.M. Monday through Friday and 1:00 to 4:00 P.M. on Saturday. For information call 332–4137.

Drive down Lander's Main Street between Sixth and Seventh streets to get a look at the enormous stack of antlers at the Fort Augur Trading Post. Try **The Magpie** at 159 North Second Street and sip coffee or tea while you partake of their delicious scones and muffins. Notice the tall false front on the building. The Magpie is open Monday through Saturday from 6:30 A.M. to 7:00 P.M. in the summer and from 7:00 A.M. to 6:00 P.M. in the winter. Call 332–5565.

For fantastic American and international cuisine complete with espresso bar, stop at the ◆**Sweetwater Grille** at 148 Main Street. The owner of the new restaurant, Paul Guschewsky, renovated a dilapidated old building into a stunning art deco dining spot. During the renovations, Paul discovered several unexpected treasures in the form of beautiful leaded stained-glass windows and a well-preserved embossed tin ceiling hidden under decades of remodeling. For reservations call 332–7388 or (800) 714–7388.

Across the street near the Popo Agie River stands a Lander landmark, the 1888 mill built by Eugene Amoretti and used to grind wheat and supply electricity for the town. It has been in continual use as a flour and feed mill since its construction.

A number of outfitters operate out of the Lander area, each with its own specialty. **Allen's Diamond Four Ranch,** a licensed professional outfitter since 1973, offers guided horseback tours by the hour or day and pack trips over 10,000-foot passes in the Popo Agie Wilderness of the Wind River Mountain Range. Pack trips last from four days to two weeks. For information call 332–2995.

Lander Llama Company provides a full line of outfitting services and pack trips aboard these adorable animals. For information and reservations call 332–5624 or (800) 582–5262.

Just outside of Lander at 2343 Baldwin Creek Road, Ed and Betty Lewis give the utmost in Western hospitality at their ◆ **Piece of Cake Bed & Breakfast.** Nestled under a bluff, the view from the Piece of Cake main house and bunkhouse cabins is terrific in every direction. You can enjoy the view from your own private bunkhouse porch. Each room is furnished in Western decor. The main house has guest quarters and kitchen complete with snacks. A unique feature is the Native American Cultural Tour hosted in conjunction with Central Wyoming College. It includes a field trip to historic Fort Washakie on the Wind River Reservation, a traditional meal prepared by Native Americans, an interpretive presentation on Sacajawea at the Shoshone Cultural Center, and a clothing and drum exhibit by Native Americans. You will learn the craft of beading from a tribe member and complete the project yourself. Other Piece of Cake events include a visit by a cowboy poet and a Western sing-along. To top it all off, the food is fantastic and plentiful. A local baker delivers fresh "Wildflour" bagels daily. Overnight rates are in the $80–$90 range. For tour and weekly rates and reservations call 332–7608 or (800) 251–6080.

An interesting place to learn about bronze art carvings and foundry work is ◆ **Eagle Bronze, Inc. Foundry & Gallery,** at 130 Poppy Street on the south edge of town in the industrial park off Highway 287. Eagle Bronze casts artwork for many of the West's famous artists. A recent coup is the largest outdoor bronze sculpture in the country, which it is preparing for the Dallas, Texas, Convention Center. *The Cattle Drive on Pioneer Plaza* consists of seventy steers and three horsemen stretching out over 180 yards. A number of the foundry's art castings are featured in the gallery and throughout Lander. Eagle Bronze offers foundry tours on Tuesdays and Thursdays at 1:30 P.M. Call 332–5436.

◆ **Sinks Canyon State Park** features a disappearing act by the Popo Agie River as it crashes and disappears into a large cavern, the Sinks, in the side of a mountain only to reappear ½ mile down the canyon in a trout-filled pool called the Rise. Two interesting facts about Sinks Canyon: First, more water comes out at the Rise than flows into the Sinks, and second, the water that flows out into the Rise is a few degrees warmer than the water entering the Sinks. A visitors center near the Sinks presents information on this unique geologic phenomenon and on area wildlife. Self-guided nature trails, picnic grounds, and overnight campsites are available on a first-come, first-served basis. Be sure to walk across the swinging bridge spanning the Popo Agie River. The visitors center is open Memorial Day through Labor Day from 9:00 A.M. to 7:00 P.M. For the athletically inclined, take the Popo Agie Falls Trail for a 1½-mile hike and be rewarded with a wonderful vista. To reach Sinks Canyon State Park, take Highway 131 southeast out of Lander for 6 miles. For information call 332–6333.

Depending on time of year, road construction, and road conditions, you can take Highway 131 on a loop through the historic mining areas of Atlantic City and South Pass City, or you can return to Lander and travel along Highway 28 south to the Atlantic City/South Pass City cutoff. It's a little more than 20 miles from Lander via Highway 28, and the road is well marked. Be sure to stop at the view turnout and look back at dramatic Red Canyon as you rise out of the valley surrounding Lander.

The first white men to discover the South Pass Route were fur traders known as the Astorians, in 1812. The pass was rediscovered by fur trapper Henry Ashley in 1824: however, Lt. John Charles Fremont is credited with widely publicizing the route over South Pass after his expedition in 1842. Through the next two and a half decades, more than 350,000 emigrants traveled up the gentle slopes headed west across the Continental Divide. In reality, South Pass, at 7,805 feet, was the key that made the Oregon Trail feasible over the mountains.

The first South Pass City was an 1850s stage stop and telegraph station where the Oregon Trail made its final crossing of the Sweetwater River. On the current site, South Pass City was built in 1867 when the discovery of gold brought a flood of prospectors to the Sweetwater Mining District. The mining boomtown flourished with the construction of three hundred buildings starting in the 1860s. The Carissa Mine began producing gold in 1867 and last worked in the 1950s. The town experienced many booms and busts through the years.

History abounds at South Pass City. This once-thriving, rough-and-tumble gold camp gave birth to the women's suffrage bill introduced to the first Territorial Legislature Assembly by South Pass City representative William Bright in November 1869. The suffrage bill passed both the council and the house on December 10, 1869, and the governor of Wyoming signed the bill into law. The territorial legislature voted to repeal the suffrage bill in 1871, but Governor Campbell vetoed this action. On another front, Esther Hobart Morris became the first woman in the United States to hold political office on February 14, 1870, when she was sworn in as justice of the peace at South Pass City. The Esther Hobart Morris historical marker and plaque are located next to the Esther Hobart Morris Cabin at South Pass City.

Today, ◆ **South Pass City State Historic Site** is one of Wyoming's largest restored historic sites, with more than thirty structures on thirty-nine acres. Footsteps echo on the wooden boardwalks and horses' hooves clop on dirt streets that lead you to an 1890 schoolhouse, the South Pass Hotel (opened as the Idaho House in 1868), the 1890s Carissa Saloon, the Riniker Cabin, and the 1870 Sweetwater County Jail. They give you a real sense of life in an 1860 gold-mining town. You can also learn how to pan gold. For a grand old time, consider attending the South Pass City Fourth of July Celebration. South Pass City is open May 15 through September 30 from 9:00 A.M. to 6:00 P.M. The entrance fee is $1.00 For information call 332–3684.

For a good view of the Oregon Trail as it approached South Pass, drive to the OREGON TRAIL–LANDER CUTOFF–SOUTH PASS AREA interpretive sign located on the south side of Highway 28 about 39 miles from Lander. You can still see where the wagon ruts cross the desert from this vantage point.

On the way back to Lander, stop at the ◆ **Atlantic City Mercantile,** located at 100 East Main Street in the semi–ghost town of Atlantic City several miles northeast of South Pass City by dirt road. You'll be able to see the remnants of buildings and other structures from the Duncan Gold Mine along the way. It's a delightful place to grab a bite to eat or spend the night at one of the A-frame guest cabins. The 103-year-old false-fronted building includes a saloon and steak house with all sorts of historic paraphernalia and photographs hanging on or nailed to the walls. Browse through the small museum and check out the

Atlantic City Mercantile

ornate antique, but still used, stove in the saloon and the set of swinging doors attached to the wall in the back room. There's a story behind every door here.

The Merc serves a barbecue on Sundays from noon to 2:00 P.M. from May 1 through November 1. Other days feature everything from a Wednesday-night Basque family-style seven-course dinner (reservations only) to good ole steaks prepared on an inside open pit fire stoked with aspen wood. In the summer you can tap your toe to lively music on Friday and Saturday nights. In the winter make it your stopover from cross-country skiing or snow-mobiling on the Continental Divide Trail. Prices are moderate. For information call 332–5143.

A United States Steel taconite strip mine (taconite is a low-grade iron ore) rejuvenated the area's economy from 1962 to

1983, but the mined-out hills are all that remain of that boom. Times are quiet once again, at least until the next boom.

The Lander area provides various outdoor sporting activities. In addition to the pack trips already mentioned, there's rock climbing in the Wild Iris Canyon, with routes ranging from 5.7 to 5.14 in difficulty. You can also enjoy the Wind River country in the wintertime. The Continental Divide Snowmobile Trail originates near Lander and ends up in Yellowstone with hundreds of miles of groomed trails running through some of the most picturesque and pristine country in the world. The staff of **Ultimate Snowmobiling Adventures** of Lander possess more than thirty combined years of snowmobiling experience on these trails and can outfit you for the trip of your life. You'll see wildlife in its natural setting and view unbelievable waterfalls and mountain range and valley vistas away from road traffic. For information call 332–9808. Moving northwest on Highway 287 out of Lander, you journey once more through Wind River Reservation territory (Riverton is located within the boundaries of the reservation). It encompasses more than two million acres and ranks as the largest reservation in the nation. Wyoming's only reservation is home to the Eastern Shoshone and the Northern Arapahoe tribes, making it the only one in the country to host two separate Native American nations.

On the reservation are the graves of three great Native American leaders: Shoshone chief Washakie, Arapahoe chief Black Coal, and Sacajawea, the Shoshone woman who traveled with Lewis and Clark on their famous 3,000-mile 1805–6 expedition. As a child, she was captured by a rival tribe and sold to French fur trader Toussaint Charbonneau, who fathered their son, Baptiste. Her ability to speak and understand English, French, and Native American languages proved invaluable on the expedition. She returned to the Shoshone people late in life and died in 1884. ◆ **Sacajawea's Grave** is located in the southwest corner of the Shoshone Cemetery at Fort Washakie about a half mile directly north of the Shoshone–Episcopal Mission sign. (Other accounts say Sacajawea died and was buried at Fort Manuel in South Dakota.) Mt. Sacajawea in the Wind River Mountains is named in her honor. There are also a number of statues of Sacajawea in Wyoming.

Shoshone chief Washakie allied himself with the white people's government as an intermediary for his people in a successful attempt at peaceful coexistence between the two peoples. He was widely recognized as an intelligent leader and his sage strategy of joining the government's forces in battles against other tribes was eventually rewarded with the presentation of large tracts of land in Colorado, Idaho, Utah, and Wyoming. Through the years, portions of the original reservation lands assigned under the Fort Bridger Treaty of 1863 were negotiated away from the Native Americans until it became the current size of the Wind River Reservation.

Chief Washakie died in 1900 on the Wind River Reservation around the age of 100. Mount Washakie and the Washakie Wilderness are named after this great Shoshone chief, as was Fort Washakie, which was renamed from Fort Brown in 1878. The post was abandoned in 1909, but the town bearing his name remains. His grave rests in the old fort cemetery. Take South Fork Road west until you come to the **Chief Washakie Gravesite.**

The Arapahoes, former Shoshone enemies, were admitted onto the Shoshone reservation in 1878 on a temporary basis. Today, there are approximately 2,500 Shoshones and 5,200 Arapahoes living on the Wind River Reservation. During summer months, residents of Wind River Reservation display their rich and colorful traditions in a variety of ways. Powwows, sundances, horseback relay races, and Native American rodeos are open to the public, as are Shoshone and Arapahoe cultural centers and some historic sites. To fish on tribal land you must first obtain a $5.00 recreation stamp issued by the Shoshone and Arapahoe Tribal Fish and Game Department at Fort Washakie. For information call the Lander Chamber of Commerce at 332–3892.

Traveling northwest 16 miles on Highway 287 and then in a more westerly direction on Highway 26/287 for about 10 miles, you'll spot a large butte on the northern horizon. Native American legend explains that the name, **Crowheart Butte,** came from an 1866 struggle to the death between Crow and Shoshone chiefs. After the Shoshone chief won, he celebrated the victory by eating the heart of his vanquished rival (or displaying the heart on his lance). The Shoshone warrior was Chief Washakie. Queried years later about the story, Chief Washakie replied, "One cannot always remember what he did when he was young and in the heat of battle."

Eleven miles before you get to Dubois, you'll want to turn right (north) onto gravel East Fork Road (Road 277) for a scenic 11-

75

mile trip up to the ◆ **Lazy L & B Ranch.** You're guaranteed a
wonderful family vacation at this hundred-year-old cattle and
guest ranch now owned by Lee and Bob Naylon. The ranch
adjoins the Wind River Reservation and an elk refuge. Bed down
in authentic long cabins (one's a schoolhouse from the homesteading area) around a central yard or alongside a babbling
stream. Down-home cooking starts with breakfast served buffet
style and lunch by the pool or on the trail. Dinner is a treat after
a day filled with activities ranging from unlimited riding to pre-
breakfast hikes up an old riverbed canyon to fly-fishing in the
stream. Three nights a week the kids eat with the wranglers and
then burn lots of energy in fun activities. Meanwhile, back at
the ranch house, the adult folks have a happy, quiet, delicious
dinner followed by evening entertainment. You can soak your
weary bones in the outdoor heated swimming pool as the setting
sun burns a brilliant crimson on the Absaroka mountain range.

The Lazy L & B Ranch was homesteaded in the 1890s by Scottish emigrants. It sits at an elevation of 7200 feet with awe-
inspiring terrain, ranging from tree-lined valley trails to the
high country, which you can see on a week of varied rides.
Anglers can fish in stocked ponds or try their luck in the East
Fork of the Wind River.

For entertainment you can listen to the ranch's own cowboy
poet or ride into Dubois for weekly square dances held at the
Rustic Pine Tavern. A special treat, National Rodeo Hall of
Famer Jared Nesset, shares his wit and wisdom with you. For the
kids, there's a petting zoo with goats, chickens, rabbits, sheep,
duck, geese, and other ranch animals. The corrals are filled with
horses and donkeys to match the skill level of any rider. Every-
body is required to go through safety training before they are
allowed to ride. The leather shop is open to kids of all ages, as is
instruction in roping techniques. Steak barbecues and bonfires
are followed by an evening of singing.

The lodge has two cozy fireplaces, a library, and game tables. All
log guest cabins have private baths or showers, electric heat, and
your very own porch from which to enjoy the evening. You can
bring your own sitter to care for two or more children at no
charge for the sitter. The season runs from the end of May
through mid-September. September is reserved for adults only.
Rates run $875 per adult and $775 per child under age twelve. Dis-

count rates are available for early- and late-season reservations. For information or reservations call 455–2839 or (800) 453–9488.

❖ **Jakey's Fork Homestead,** located 4 miles east of Dubois off Forest Service Road 411 south of Highway 26/287, provides the unique experience of sleeping in the homestead cabin and bunkhouse with the water of Jakey's Fork flowing within feet of your bedroom window. It's hard to imagine a more peaceful setting or a more restful evening. In the morning you can explore the homestead with its sod-roofed buildings and the mountains and the badlands in the distance. The main house facility has a shared guest bathroom with Jacuzzi and cypress- and redwood-lined sauna.

Breakfast is served on the second floor of the main house in a dining space with windows on three sides offering unobstructed views of the Wind River Mountains. Sourdough pancakes and elk sausage, along with plenty of fruit and biscuits or Scottish oat scones, will satisfy your appetite. Owners Irene and Justin Bridges have created numerous lush flower and rock gardens to enjoy from the deck. Jakey's Fork is a blue-ribbon trout stream and flows through the property for ½ mile.

The hundred-year-old barn houses Justin's knife workshop. A founding member of the Professional Knife Makers Association, Justin handcrafts fine sporting knives and kitchen cutlery under his Wind River Knives brand and is happy to demonstrate his craft. He made the Wyoming Centennial Knife for the governor. The telephone number for the knife shop is 455–2769.

The surrounding area offers plenty of things to do, from white-water rafting on the Wind River to scenic drives through the badlands. Nearby Trail Road (Road 257) offers views of bighorn sheep, osprey nests, waterfalls, and petroglyphs. The road leads to Glacier Trail and the three glacial lakes of Torrey, Ring, and Trail. Rates at Jakey's Fork Homestead are $65 per evening per couple or $60 for a single in the main house and $50 and up per evening for the rustic homestead cabin. Ask Irene to tell the story about Butch Cassidy chasing away renegade Indians from the homestead. For information and reservations call 455–2769.

Within walking distance of the bed and breakfast is the **Dubois Fish Hatchery,** which has been in operation since 1930. The area's abundant natural spring water is important for successful fish rearing. The Lake of the Woods brood stock, obtained about 30 miles southwest of Dubois, furnishes a major portion of the cutthroat eggs for the entire state. The hatchery also raises rainbow trout, grayling, and golden, brook, and brown trout, depending on the state's requirements. Rainbow trout make up approximately 60 percent of the hatchery's annual production. The hatchery's three incubators are capable of handling up to six million eggs at one time. The informative hatchery tour takes you from egg fertilization through fish planting. The fish hatchery is located at Five Fish Hatchery Court. For information call 455-2431.

Dubois (population 895), located just 5 miles west on Highway 26/287, has kept its Western flavor despite a lot of remodeling in recent years. Boardwalk sidewalks and false-fronted stores abound. The town grew up around a post office established on Horse Creek more than a century ago. The newest addition to the town is the **◆ National Bighorn Sheep Interpretive Center,** completed in 1993. It contains educational exhibits on bighorn sheep biology, habitat protection, and herd management techniques being employed at the Whiskey Mountain Wildlife Habitat Management Area several miles east of town. Dubois is a natural location for the interpretive center since the area is home to North America's largest population of Rocky Mountain bighorn sheep. The center came about through the cooperative efforts of the U.S. Forest Service, U.S. Bureau of Land Management, Wyoming Game and Fish Department, Town of Dubois, and private individuals and organizations.

The central exhibit, a 16-foot-tall "sheep mountain," puts full-size bighorns in their natural environment. Interpretive scenes depicting predator–prey relationships, lambing areas, and dominance fights ring the slopes of the mountain. Children young and old will be fascinated by all of the informative hands-on displays. A gift shop sells nature books, posters and cards, wildlife-theme clothing, prints, sculptures, and antler art crafted by local artisans. For fall and winter travelers, there's a special treat. You can take your own four-wheel-drive vehicle or sign up for a guided tour of winter wildlife in the Whiskey Mountain habitat area sponsored by the National Bighorn Sheep Interpretive Center. November is the best time to view rutting. The tour starts at 9:00 A.M. and lasts approximately five hours. The guide vehicle seats six people. Binoculars and sporting scopes are provided, but you are responsible for your own lunch and hot beverage. Be sure to dress appropriately. The tours begin in mid-November and continue through March.

The National Bighorn Sheep Interpretive Center is located at 907 West Ramshorn off Highway 26/287. Hours from Memorial Day weekend to Labor Day weekend are 9:00 A.M. to 8:00 P.M. daily and during the winter on Thursday through Monday from 9:00 A.M. to 4:00 P.M. Entrance fees are $2.00 per adult, 75 cents per child age twelve and under, or $5.00 per family. For information on the center or the winter wildlife tours, call 455–3429.

Right next door at 909 West Ramshorn, the **Dubois Museum** exhibits focus on the Sheepeater Indians and the area's ranch and frontier life, and the timber industry's historical importance to Dubois. The sawmill shut down in 1987, resulting in community leaders putting more emphasis on tourism and economic draws such as the National Bighorn Sheep Interpretive Center. The museum is open daily from Memorial Day to Labor Day, 9:00 A.M. to 5:00 P.M. For information call 455–2284.

For a gourmet tune-up pull into the ◆ **Old Yellowstone Garage,** a new Western/Italian ristorante on the main drag. The owners arrived in Dubois from northern Italy. The restaurant features a new menu every day. Choose from a wide variety of dishes, from grilled endive and eggplant as an appetizer before you dive into a second course of homemade pasta, to a main course of grilled boneless trout, grilled double-cut pork chops, or charred stuffed chicken. The barbecue eatery in the building out back is also part of the same operation. For information call 455–3666.

Not far away, at 120 East Ramshorn, **Stewart's Trapline Gallery and Indian Trading Post** stocks a fine collection of original paintings and bronze sculptures by co-owner Mark R. Stewart. Kit and Mark Stewart carry an extensive collection of traditional Native American art representing more than twenty-six tribes. Choose a treasure for your home from a variety of art forms, such as High Plains artifacts, beadwork, old pottery and basketry, sand paintings, Navajo rugs, Kachina Dolls, Zuni fetishes, and contemporary Native American silver jewelry. For information call 455–2800.

A number of self-guided loop tours out of Dubois are worth considering. You have your choice of viewing the badlands up close or journeying to a series of three glacial lakes for great fishing or viewing wildlife and wildflowers in the mountain meadows. Native American petroglyphs are within easy access for photographing. The largest glacial and snow fields in the continental United States and Wyoming's highest mountain, Gannett Peak, are all within a several hour's drive from Dubois. Pick up a map outlining "Six Loop Tour Options" in the Wind River Country tourist pubication, available at the Dubois Chamber of Commerce office at 616 West Ramshorn, or call 455–2556.

Driving northwest from Dubois on Highway 26/287 you'll come upon the **Union Pass Monument** about 8 miles out. This marks the first road across the Absarokas. The 9,210-foot Union Pass also creates an interesting natural phenomenon. It is the only place in the United States where rivers flow in three different directions. The Roaring Fork winds its way to the Colorado River, Jakey's Fork flows to the Mississippi River, while Fisk Creek eventually drains into the Columbia River. Union Pass also separates three mountain ranges: the Absarokas heading into Montana, the Gros Ventre moving southwesterly, and the Wind Rivers taking a southeasterly direction. You can take the Union Pass Road for a delightful trip to Pinedale past breathtaking mountain scenery.

Drive another 9 miles down the highway and you'll reach an impressive carved stone called the ◆**Tie Hack Monument.** It's near the site of the first tie camp on the Wind River. Tie hackers cut some 400,000 railroad ties annually here between 1914 and 1946. The ties were then moved along the Wind River during the spring runoff. The lumberjacks precariously rode the ties downriver, an operation that lasted several wet weeks. Many of them suffered from an ailment called "squeak heel," caused by having continuously wet feet. Eventually, their Achilles tendons would dry out and squeak.

Tie hackers had to cut a tie to a precise 7 inches per side to pass close inspection. For this they earned 10 cents a tie or up to $3.00 a day, while their room and board cost $1.50 per day. Each tie hacker cared for his own equipment, which cost him about ten days' pay to acquire. It was said that the Scandinavian tie hackers "could plane logs so smooth with an ax that one could run a hand across them without picking up a single splinter."

Ahead of you lies the beginning of the Wyoming Centennial Scenic Byway leading to Togwotee Pass (elevation 9,658 feet) and down into Teton Valley and the Bridger-Teton National Forests. That journey will be covered in the Western Wyoming section of this book. For now, the drive alternates between mountain meadows, lodgepole forests, and towering cliffs.

NORTHERN WYOMING

39
Cody 38
37 • 36
35
31 30
Sheridan 12
13 • Sheridan
14
15 17 16
18
10
Crook
Park
34
33
Big Horn 29
11
Campbell
2
1
3
23
• Worland
Washakie
19
21 20
9 •
Gillette
Weston
5
4
6
Hot Springs
28 27
25 24
26
Johnson
22
8
7
32

1. Aladdin General Store
2. Devils Tower National Monument
3. Crook County Museum and Art Gallery
4. Cambria
5. Flying V Cambria Inn
6. Anna Miller Museum
7. Coal Mine Tours
8. Durham Buffalo Ranch
9. Campbell County Rockpile Museum
10. Recluse Branch Library
11. RBL Bison Ranch
12. Sheridan Inn
13. Trail End Historic Center
14. Bradford Brinton Memorial
15. Spahn's Big Horn Bed & Breakfast
16. Fetterman Massacre Monument
17. Wagon Box Fight
18. Fort Phil Kearny
19. Jim Gatchell Museum of the West
20. Cloud Peak Inn

21. Crazy Woman Canyon
22. Outlaw Cave
23. Trail of the Whispering Giants
24. Hot Springs State Park
25. Broadway Inn Bed & Breakfast
26. Wind River Canyon
27. Legend Rock Petroglyph Site
28. High Island Ranch & Cattle Company
29. Medicine Lodge State Archaeological Site
30. Medicine Wheel
31. Bighorn Canyon National Recreation Area
32. Museum of Flight and Aerial Firefighting
33. Charles J. Belden Museum
34. Broken Spoke Cafe and Bed & Breakfast
35. Cody Guest Houses
36. Buffalo Bill Historical Center
37. Buffalo Bill Dam
38. Homesteader's Museum
39. Chief Joseph Scenic Highway

NORTHERN WYOMING

CROOK COUNTY

Entering northern Wyoming on Interstate 90 from South Dakota, you'll want to take a little diversion north on Highway 111 to Aladdin. The town takes its name from the character in *Arabian Nights* who rubbed the lamp and released two jinn (genie). It was chosen by the California capitalist who laid out the town as a rail stop for the Wyoming and Missouri Valley Railroad.

While there may not be any genie in Aladdin, the town does possess its own magic. Spend a pleasant hour or two at the ✦ **Aladdin General Store.** Besides serving the local area with groceries and hardware, it operates as the post office and community center where the issues of the day are discussed. The general store also encompasses a neat little museum. The structure housing the Aladdin General Store was built by Bill Robinson in 1896 as a saloon. The building is listed on the National Register of Historic Places. So is a mine tipple from the late 1880s coal-mining ventures 2½ miles east of town. It is one of the few remaining historic tipples in Wyoming.

In Aladdin's Antique Attic, which is part of the general store, you'll discover antique furniture, blankets, rugs, books, and Western art. As they say in Aladdin, "grab a refreshment and kick back on the front porch." The Aladdin General Store is open daily Monday through Saturday from 8:00 A.M. until 6:00 P.M. in the winter and until 7:00 P.M. in the summer, and on Sunday from 10:00 A.M. to 5:00 P.M. in the winter and 9:00 A.M. to 6:00 P.M. during the summer. For information call 896–2226.

Just as a point of reference, the lowest point in Wyoming is located in Crook County, at an elevation of 3,125 feet as the Belle Fourche River enters the state 10 miles northeast of Aladdin. Wyoming has the second highest mean elevation in the United States at 6,700 feet.

Crook County was named after famous Indian fighter General George Crook. Another, less fortunate Indian fighter, General George A. Custer traveled through Crook County leading the first government expedition to search for gold in the Black Hills of South Dakota and Wyoming. You can still make out remnants of Custer's July 1874 trail as more than one hundred wagons and a force of one thousand troops, engineers, geologists and miners crossed the terrain. There's a Custer Expedition sign about 3 miles west of Aladdin on the south side of Highway 24.

For the most part, the 1876 Black Hills gold rush stayed on the South Dakota side of the border. A few abandoned "glory holes" are located around the Aladdin area. The Black Hills of Wyoming deliver a treasure of another kind. The route along the Bear Lodge Mountains as you head west on Highway 24 gives you a mother lode of beautiful scenery. You'll discover lofty sandstone cliffs, red hills, flower-filled meadows, pristine creeks and rivers, and clusters of ponderosa pine, cedar and oak. Along the way, you can picnic at the Bearlodge campground, located 7 miles west of Aladdin, or at any of the other campgrounds in the Black Hills National Forest.

Proceed through Alva and follow Highway 24 southwest at Hulett to reach ❖ **Devils Tower National Monument.** President Theodore Roosevelt designated Devils Tower as the nation's first national monument in 1906. The first documented white men to view Devils Tower were members of Captain W. F. Raynold's 1859 Yellowstone expedition. Colonel Richard I. Dodge led a U.S. Geologic Survey expedition to the unique formation in 1875. A Devils Tower plaque is located on the east wall of the visitors center.

Geologists still argue whether Devils Tower is the result of a volcanic core exposed after millions of years of erosion or molten rock forced upward from the bowels of the earth through existing rock layers. The rocks and boulders at its base are broken pieces of columns shed from the core.

The most popular of the Mateo Tipi or Bear Lodge (Devils Tower) Indian legends involves the story of a bear chasing seven maidens. The girls jumped upon a rock several feet high and prayed, "Rock, save us." Hearing the pleas of the girls, the rock began to elongate itself upwards, pushing them higher and higher, out of the clutches of the bear. The bear clawed at the sides of the rock, which continued to grow until it reached the sky. The claw marks are there to this day. As for the seven Indian maidens, they are the seven stars making up the constellation Pleiades (in Greek mythology these seven stars are the daughters of Atlas).

In any event, Devils Tower is a magnificent sight, rising 865 feet. The top spreads out to a 180-by-300-foot oval. At the base

Devils Tower

there is a paved 1¼-mile walking path around the rock perimeter. Nearby, a large prairie dog town will keep you and the kids occupied as the furry critters vie for your attention with a variety of amusing antics.

The strange geological phenomenon made it to the big screen in Hollywood's production of *Close Encounters of the Third Kind*. Devils Tower has also drawn a lot of attention recently because of the number of rock climbers scaling its sheer cliffs. Wyoming rancher William Rogers became the first to reach the top of the formation on July 4, 1893, using wooden pegs he pounded into crevices in the rock face. Modern rock climbing techniques were not used to climb the tower until 1936 when Fritz Wiessner and other members of the American Alpine Club made the ascent.

Efforts are presently under way to restrict the number of climbs annually in deference to Devils Tower's role as a sacred Native American site.

Try to be at the tower around sunset for a spectacular view. It's impossible to describe the scene with justice, so we won't even try.

Devils Tower National Monument is open year-round; however, the campground, restaurants, and gift shops operate on a seasonal basis. Inquire at the visitors center about special programs and interpretive presentations. The center is open daily from 8:00 A.M. to 4:45 P.M. with extended hours during the summer months. There is a minimal entrance fee per vehicle. The center is located 10 miles south of Hulett on Highway 24 and then west 3 miles on a paved park road. For information call 467–5370.

Moorcroft (population 768) is located on the banks of the Belle Fourche River. From Devils Tower take Highway 24 south to Devils Tower Junction and then Highway 14 headed southwest. All told it's about 32 miles. The town served as a major railhead for cattle shipments from the large ranch spreads headquartered here. In addition, the Texas Cattle Trail moved thousands of cattle through the Moorcroft area in the 1880s and 1890s. In 1891 Moorcroft ranked as the leading cattle shipping point in the country. **The Western Texas Trail Museum** in downtown Moorcroft captures the thrill of the cattle drive and the area's ranching history. The museum is located at 220 South Big Horn. It is open daily from 1:00 to 4:00 P.M. May through September.

As you drove down to Moorcroft from Devils Tower you undoubtedly noticed the Keyhole Reservoir on your right. From **Keyhole State Park** you can peer at Devils Tower beyond your crackling campfire. The park's fourteen thousand acres of water provide plenty of boating, fishing, swimming, and bird-watching opportunities. The reservoir is a mecca for 225 species of birds. Be on the lookout for bald eagles, common yellow-throat, osprey, wild turkeys, and white pelicans. Park headquarters has a complete bird list.

From Memorial Day through Labor Day you can walk the park's 6.2-mile official volksmarch trail. Nearby Pine Haven's recreation board sponsors a 5K run from Pine Haven into Keyhole State Park. The park was named after the "keyhole brand" used by the McKean Ranch. The park entrance is situated on the south side of the reservoir and is accessible off Highway 113. Entrance fees are several dollars per vehicle. A full-service marina, motel, and cafe are located on Headquarters Road, adjacent to the lakeshore. For information call 756–3596.

The largest community and our last stop in Crook County is Sundance (population 1,139). From Keyhole State Park follow Pine Ridge Road south 8 miles to Interstate 90. Take the interstate east 22 miles to the Sundance exit. Most famous for giving Harry Longabaugh (alias "The Sundance Kid") his nickname, the town boasts a number of other attractions. In the ◆ **Crook County Museum and Art Gallery,** you can see the original furniture from the courtroom where the Sundance Kid was tried and convicted of horse thieving. He made the grave mistake of stealing a slow horse. The misadventure cost Longabaugh eighteen months in jail but gained him a catchy alias.

Other museum displays include cowboy gear, branding irons, a re-creation of a prehistoric buffalo jump, and Native American artifacts. The art gallery exhibits works by Crook County artists and photographers. Summer hours are 8:00 A.M. to 8:00 P.M. Monday through Friday and 9:00 A.M. to 4:00 P.M. Saturday. Off-season hours are 8:00 A.M. to 5:00 P.M. Monday through Friday. The museum and art gallery are located in the lower level of the Crook County Courthouse on Cleveland Street. For information call 283–3666.

The town sits below Sundance Mountain (its Sioux name is *Wi Wacippi Paha,* meaning Temple of the Sioux), where Sioux Indians performed sacred sun dances. These religious dances represented the triumph of good over evil and the beginning of life. The sun dance ritual lasted from several days to weeks and many Native Americans traveled to Wi Wacippi Paha to observe the ceremony.

WESTON COUNTY

Newcastle (population 3,003) lies along the Cheyenne–Black Hills Stage Route, only 10 miles from the South Dakota border via Highway 16. Burlington Northern coal trains from Wyoming's massive mines in coal-rich Thunder Basin also roll through the town, proving you can at least haul coal through, if not to, Newcastle. The town was founded as a coal-mining and shipping center and named after its more famous sister city Newcastle-upon-Tyne, the great English coal port.

One of the town's attractions is actually outside of town at the ghost town site of ◆ **Cambria,** once a thriving Burlington and Missouri River Railroad coal town with a population of 1,500 people comprising twenty-three separate nationalities. From the 1880s through 1928, Cambria supplied the nation with thirteen million tons of western coal. There is a **Cambria Mining Camp Marker** located a little more than 5 miles north of Newcastle on the west side of Highway 85. The ghost town site is approximately 5 miles west of the sign, located on private property. Inquire at the Newcastle Chamber of Commerce (800–835–0157) for permission from the property owner to view the Cambria site.

Three miles further north on Highway 85 you arrive at the ◆ **Flying V Cambria Inn.** The Cambria Flying V Casino opened in 1928, months before the mines closed for good. It now houses a bed and breakfast and restaurant in a beautiful hills setting. The Tudor castle–like structure is listed on the National Register of Historic Places. The restaurant specializes in Italian food, fish, and steaks and serves dinner only. It is closed from January through May. Prices are moderate. For information or reservations call 746–2096.

Back in town, the ◆ **Anna Miller Museum** has an abundant collection of material on Cambria and many artifacts from this international melting pot. The museum is housed in one of the last Army National Guard cavalry stables, built in the 1930s and listed on the National Register of Historic Places. Browse through collections of fossils, 1890 firefighting equipment, a country store and pioneer doctor's office, and various types of horse-drawn transportation. Outside you can see the 1890–1930 Green Mountain Schoolhouse and the early 1900s Novak Miller Cabin. The museum is located at Delaware and Washington Park off Highway 16. Off-season hours are 9:00 A.M. to 5:00 P.M. Monday through Friday, Thursday evenings until 7:00 P.M. June through August hours are Monday through Friday from 9:00 A.M. to 7:00 P.M., and Saturday 1:00 to 5:00 P.M. For information call 746–4188.

On the north side of Main Street east of the railroad tracks, there's a sign marking THE HANGING OF DIAMOND L. SLIM CLIFTON. Clifton was lynched in 1903 after the murder of his neighbors, Louella and John Church. An angry mob stormed the jail and took Clifton from the sheriff at gunpoint. He was hanged from the railroad bridge, which has since been removed.

For a bite to eat before leaving Weston County, consider stopping at the **Old Mill Inn** at 500 West Main Street. As indicated by its name, the structure once operated as the town flour mill. Hours are 5:00 A.M. to 11:00 P.M. daily. For information call 746–2711.

CAMPBELL COUNTY

Campbell County is coal country. Behemoth draglines load 240-ton trucks with coal from the Black Thunder Coal Mine near Wyoming's newest community, Wright (population 1,236). To reach the heart of the nation's largest deposit of low-sulphur coal, take Highway 450 west from Newcastle 66 miles until it dead-ends into Highway 59. Take this road 2 miles north until you reach Wright. Along Highway 450 you will pass through the Thunder Basin National Grassland. In all, the grasslands cover some two million acres set aside by the federal government for soil conservation and preservation. The Powder River Coal Basin contains an estimated 1 trillion short tons of in-place coal reserves. There are seventeen coal mines in the area, some of which provide tours. For information on ❖ **Coal Mine Tours,** call Thunder Basin Coal Company at 939–1300, extension 294.

Although the town was founded in 1976 and incorporated in 1985, it has already put together a unique museum. The **Wright Centennial Museum** has an interesting collection covering not only coal mining but also World War I memorabilia and pioneer farm implements. Outside the museum sits a seventy-ton truck that was retired in 1990. The museum is open May 15 to October 20 on Monday through Friday from 10:00 A.M. to 5:00 P.M. Wright Centennial Museum is located at 104 Ranch Court. For information call 939–1261.

Tours are also in the offing at the ❖ **Durham Buffalo Ranch.** With more than 3,000 head, it's one of the largest private buffalo herds. The buffalo or American bison, ranks high with Wyomingites. It takes a prominent position on the state flag and is the state mammal. Weighing up to two tons, the buffalo is the largest North American land mammal. At one time, more than seventy-five million of these majestic beasts roamed the prairies and high plains. Millions were slaughtered for food and sport in the late 1800s. Hunters such as "Buffalo Bill" Cody earned their reputations supplying railroad crews with buffalo meat and hides. By the time Congress passed the first federal protection legislation for buffalo in 1894, their numbers had dwindled to less than one thousand in all of North America. The disappearance of the buffalo affected the Native Americans, who relied on them for food, clothing, shelter cooking utensils, tools, weapons, and fuel.

Today, the buffalo is enjoying a resurrection with more than 70,000 scattered across the country in herds ranging from several hundred to several thousand. Since this animal is no longer endangered, don't hesitate to eat a buffalo steak or buffalo burger. They taste great and are very lean.

The Durham Buffalo Ranch is located on Highway 59 about 8 miles north of Wright and encompasses more than 55,000 acres. To arrange a tour call 939–1271.

Now it's time to head north on Highway 59 through the wide-open spaces to Gillette. The town was named after railroad surveyor Edward Gillette, who laid out the track line of the Burlington and Missouri River Railroad through Gillette to Sheridan before it crosses the border into Montana. Edward Gillette was credited with saving the railroad 5 miles of track and thirty bridges in the Campbell County area by routing the track through the spot where the town of Gillette arose soon after. The town was incorporated in 1891, a year after the track was laid.

Like Wright, Gillette's existence centers around the coal industry. The boom in coal production has made Gillette the state's fifth largest city with a population of 17,635, more than half of Campbell County's 29,370 people. The wealth deriving from coal has paid off with impressive cultural facilities. Campbell County Public Library houses an extensive collection of books on Wyoming and an impressive collection of art by well-known artists. You can also visit a planetarium, 960-seat theater, and the Cam-Plex Heritage Center Gallery. Call (800) 544–6136.

The **Campbell County Public Library,** at 2102 4-J Road, features a unique outside sculpture, the *Sheepherders' Monument,* with bronze sculptures by a noted regional artist and an original "stone johnny" (sheepherder's stone marker) moved from a nearby ranch. Later we'll stop at the Recluse Branch Library in a 1934 log building. The Campbell County Public Library is open Monday through Thursday 9:00 A.M. to 9:00 P.M. and Friday and Saturday 9:00 A.M. to 5:00 P.M.

A real treat is the ◆ **Campbell County Rockpile Museum,** located at 900 West Second Street. You'll see a fine collection of pioneer vehicles such as a chuck wagon, sheep wagon, and horse-drawn hearse. Black horses pulling the hearse signaled that a man was to be buried, while gray horses indicated that a woman or child had died. Also on display are hand-tooled saddlery, branding irons, barbed wire, and Native American artifacts including arrowheads. Outside, there's a one-room schoolhouse with a woodstove and no indoor plumbing. Of course, you'll also learn about railroading and coal mining. The museum is open June 1 through August 31 on Monday through Saturday from 9:00 A.M. to 8:00 P.M. and on Sunday from 12:30 to 6:30 P.M. During the rest of the year, hours are 9:00 A.M. to 5:00 P.M. Monday through Saturday. For information call 682–5723.

If you missed the coal mine tour at Wright or still have the need to see more, call the Gillette Convention and Visitors Bureau at (800) 544–6136. Or you can drive out to the **Wyodak Overlook** to get an overview of a coal mine in operation. To reach the overlook take Highway 14/16. The overlook is next to the highway 5 miles east of Gillette. The Wyodak Mine first opened in 1922, and is the oldest operating coal mine in the Powder River Basin. It still produces nearly three million tons of coal annually, half of which is burned at the adjacent **Wyodak Power Plant.** You can also tour this 330-megawatt power plant, which burns coal to generate steam that in turn is converted into electricty. Power plant tours are conducted on Monday through Friday 9:00 A.M. to 3:00 P.M. For information contact the Gillette Convention and Visitor's Bureau at 314 South Gillette Avenue or call 686–0040 or (800) 544–6136.

You can enjoy a variety of eating experiences in town. For Chinese American cooking try the **Hong Kong Restaurant** (682–5829) at 1612 West Second Street; for homemade specialties try **Bailey's Bar & Grill** (686–7678) at 301 South Gillette Avenue; and for Mexican food visit **Casa Del Re** (682–4738) at 409 West Second Street. Food prices are moderate at all three restaurants.

Nature lovers will love **McManamen Park** for its excellent bird-watching. The park is designed to simulate waterfowl habitat. Benches and viewing blinds are available for up-close bird-watching. McManamen Park is located between Brooks Street and Gurley Street along Warlow Drive on the north side of Gillette.

Once you have finished your bird-watching, take Warlow Drive west and then head northwest on Highway 14/16 to Recluse, 38 miles away. The drive will take you through some of the best and most scenic ranching territory in Wyoming. Recluse was established in 1918 as a post office and was given its name because of the great distances between area ranches and the post office. As mentioned earlier, the ❖ **Recluse Branch Library** of the Campbell County Public Library system is interesting. It is located in the Recluse Community Hall and consists of a wall cupboard that is opened to allow patrons to peruse the collection. The library was first organized in 1927 as The Pleasant Hour Club and was moved into the Community Hall in 1934. The log building was constructed with logs cut and hauled by area residents.

Stop for a photo op at **Spotted Horse;** the whole town is wrapped up in a combination bar, cafe, and gas station. It's located on Highway 14/16 just before you leave Campbell County and enter Sheridan County. The community is named after a Cheyenne chief.

SHERIDAN COUNTY

By now, the Big Horn Mountains and the Big Horn National Forest are taking over the horizon. Between Leiter and Clearmont on Highway 14/16 you have another opportunity to view bison grazing, on the ❖ **RBL Bison Ranch.** Tours are $5.00 per person and take place daily at 2:00 P.M. from May through September. The ranch has had some prize bison such as T.J., a gold trophy winner at the National Western Livestock Show in Denver, and Tiny, T.J.'s father and the largest domestic bison ever known to be weighed in the United States and Canada. Tiny stood 6 feet, 6 inches tall and weighed 2,700 pounds. The bison ranch also features a restaurant serving buffalo meat and a gift shop with buffalo items. The ranch's bed-and-breakfast cabins run $78 per evening for a double. For information call 758–4387 or (800) 597–0109.

John D. Loucks plotted Sheridan in 1882, naming it after his Civil War commanding officer, General Philip Sheridan. The Burlington and Missouri River Railroad came to town ten years later. To its credit, Sheridan kept most of its downtown buildings intact and the entire Main Street district has been designated a

National Historic Landmark. It has the largest collection of original buildings from the late 1800s and early 1900s in Wyoming.

Established in 1893, the ◆ **Sheridan Inn** was built by the Burlington and Missouri River Railroad. Buffalo Bill Cody led the Grand March from the dining room at the opening of the inn on June 23. The W. F. Cody Hotel Company, of which Buffalo Bill was a part-owner, managed the inn from 1894 to 1902. Buffalo Bill first performed his famous Wild West Show in 1870, headlining such stars as Annie Oakley and Sitting Bull. When in town, Buffalo Bill sat on the porch of the Sheridan Inn and auditioned acts for the upcoming season.

Hand-hewn beams span the entire dining area. The ornate bar in the inn's Buffalo Bill Saloon came from England by boat, by rail to Gillette, and by ox-drawn wagon the rest of the way. The lobby's counter, stone fireplace, and cigar case are all original. The inn had electric lights when it opened and was touted as the finest establishment between Chicago and San Francisco. Its two bathtub rooms were the first in the area. Room and board could be had for the princely sum of $2.50 per day.

Architect Thomas Kimball modeled the inn after a hunting lodge he had visited in Scotland. It featured 14-foot-wide porches that circled the entire building and was highlighted in "Ripley's Believe It or Not" as "The House of 69 Gables." Famous visitors at the hotel included Calamity Jane, Ernest Hemingway, General Jack Pershing, Will Rogers, Charlie Russell, and Presidents Hoover, Taft, and Teddy Roosevelt.

The Sheridan Inn was designated a National Historic Landmark in 1964. It ceased to operate as a hotel in 1965 and is now in the process of restoration under the Sheridan Inn Joint Powers Board. Once again it serves as a social gathering spot. The inn is located at Fifth Street and Broadway. For information call 674-5440.

The mansion of senator, governor, and rancher John B. Kendrick (known as the Sagebrush Senator) offers another wonderful way to spend a few hours. Kendrick served as governor of Wyoming from 1914 to 1916 and as a U.S. senator from 1916 until his death in 1933. Now called the ◆ **Trail End Historic Center,** the 1913 structure employed Flemish-revival architecture, a rarity in the West. The house contained a number of devices that were innovative for its time. An intercom system functioned throughout the house, a dumbwaiter moved between

Sheridan Inn

floors, and a stationary vacuum system with a motor in the basement helped ease the staff's workload.

Machine-tooled woodwork and a hand-painted ceiling embellish the grand foyer. Stained-glass windows, a white Italian marble fireplace, French silk damask wall coverings, and large Oriental rugs welcome visitors. A self-guided tour booklet leads you through the mansion. Also noteworthy on site is a log cabin that served as the first post office, store, law office, and bank in the city of Sheridan. The grounds are beautifully decorated with flower beds, and a plant identification list is available. The Kendrick ranches of northern Wyoming and southern Montana encompassed more than 200,000 acres. The Trail End Historic Center is located at 400 East Clarendon Avenue. It is open daily between Memorial Day and Labor Day from 9:00 A.M. to 5:00 P.M. and the rest of the year Tuesday through Saturday 9:00 A.M. to 5:00 P.M. For information call 674–4589.

Don King, founder of **King's Ropes and Saddlery,** started handcrafting saddles and tooling saddle leather more than a half century ago. He has passed along the operation to the next generation, and his handiwork is still much in evidence in the combination store and museum at 184 North Main Street. Likewise, some of the younger fellas have picked up a thing or two from the old pro over the years. Whether you only need to outfit yourself in a King's cap or are looking to saddle up, King's is the place for quality ropes, saddles, and accessories. The museum collection includes an interesting array of spurs, chaps, and, of course, saddles. Hours are 8:00 A.M. to 5:00 P.M. Monday through Saturday. For information call 672–2702.

For great Italian food with an intimate atmosphere, chow down at **Ciao's.** The food is delicious and the prices are moderate to expensive. Ciao's is located at 120 North Main Street. For reservations call 672–2838. For local flavor visit **The Mint** at 151 North Main Street. This famous watering hole gives you an authentic taste of the West with Charles Belden photographs, stuffed critters, cattle brands, and real cowboys. Call 674–9696.

A short drive puts you in the heart of the Big Horn Mountains. Before you depart, pick up a copy of the *Big Horn Mountain Country Map* for a listing of campsites and other attractions along the Big Horn Scenic Byways. Copies are available at the Sheridan County Chamber of Commerce in Sheridan at Fifth Street and Interstate 90. For information call 672–2485.

Take Interstate 90 west 11 miles to Ranchester. Here you'll find the **Connor Battlefield** in the city park along the Tongue River bottomland. It marks a major military engagement of the Powder River Expedition in 1865. General Patrick E. Connor's forces attacked and destroyed Arapahoe Chief Black Bear's village of 250 lodges. Today the battlefield is a peaceful picnic and hiking area. Cross over the river on the cable footbridge for additional hiking paths.

The **Pegasus Gallery,** at 629 Dayton Road, has a quality selection of Native American and Western artwork from antler art to dreamcatchers. According to Native American legend, a dreamcatcher is a circular piece of art with a web that catches your good dreams as you sleep and lets the bad dreams pass through. Call 655–9226 or (800) 529–9343.

Continuing on Highway 14 to Dayton you'll first pass the **Sawyer Battlefield,** where Colonel J. A. Sawyer's men fought Indians for thirteen straight days before General Connor's troops came to the rescue. On Main Street in Dayton there's the **cabin of Hans Kleiber,** a famous naturalist artist. A number of his paintings are located at the Bradford Brinton Memorial, which we'll visit in Big Horn later. Another interesting site, located in the city park, is the **Dayton Bell Tower,** built in 1910 and used by residents as an observation point during World War II. In 1911 Dayton became the first community in Wyoming to elect a woman mayor. Dayton mayor Susan Wissler was the first woman mayor in America to serve two consecutive terms. She also operated a millinery and dry goods store and taught in the local school.

Follow Highway 14 toward Shell Canyon for some beautiful vistas. Alongside the road, signs indicate the geologic age of the rocks. Look for the rock formation called Steamboat Point and the massive rock slide areas of **Fallen City** and Buffalo Tongue Mountain (also called Horseshoe Mountain); they are real treats. For safety reasons, wait for a road turnout before you stop to take photographs. Don't worry, there are frequent turnouts.

The Big Horn Scenic Byways are especially stunning decked out in their colorful autumn foliage. Travel on Highway 14 is open year-round, with occasional closures due to winter weather. Highway 14A is open from approximately mid-May through mid-November. Elevations on the three byways range from 4,800 feet to over 9,600 feet. On a clear day you'll be able to see Devils Tower rising beyond Sheridan Valley. The switchbacks on Highway 14 bring you to named geologic formations such as Amsden, Chugwater, Gros Ventre, and Tensleep. You're guaranteed to experience an abundance of wildflowers and wildlife. More than 265 species of birds make the Big Horns their home. The namesake bighorn sheep, mule deer, elk, and moose make their presence known frequently along the byways.

Traveling south of Sheridan, forsake Interstate 90 for the more picturesque Highway 87 and then Highway 335 to Big Horn. The area is home to one of the oldest polo clubs in the United States. The Big Horn Equestrian Center, on Bird Farm Road south of Big Horn, schedules polo matches every Sunday afternoon from May to September. The Center also sponsors steeplechase races, dressage competitions, steer roping events, and soccer tournaments. There's a strong British influence in the area, where many early ranches were begun by titled English families.

The **Big Horn Store** is a general mercantile store that takes you back to a much simpler time. Built in 1882, it's one of the oldest businesses in northern Wyoming.

The ◆ **Bradford Brinton Memorial** at 239 Brinton Road in Big Horn, is an informative and worthwhile stop. The property is on the National Register of Historic Places and lies on the internationally recognized Quarter Circle A Ranch. William and Malcolm Moncreiffe built the original homestead in 1892. Bradford Brinton purchased the property in 1923 and raised Thoroughbred horses on the ranchland. He enlarged the house to its present size of twenty rooms.

Brinton loved the West and amassed a significant collection of more than 600 original oils, watercolors, and sketches by American artists. Many well-known Western artists were among his friends and visited his ranch. The collection includes works by by John J. Audubon, Edward M. Borein, E. W. Gollings, Will James, Hans Kleiber, Frederic Remington, and Charles M. Russell. The art is found in both the gallery and the ranch homestead. Tours are provided through the two-story white neo-Colonial ranch house.

In addition to paintings, the gallery showcases an excellent array of Native American handicrafts and clothing items, such as a painted steerhide dance shield, baby cradleboards, a Cree saddle cushion, Sioux ceremonial dress, and a Nez Perce buckskin shirt. Other attractions include a Jefferson Peace Medal dated 1861, which was given to a Native American chief by Lewis and Clark, and an Abraham Lincoln letter dated 1848.

Original art found in the homestead includes Charles M. Russell's bronze sculpture titled *The Bucker and the Buckeroo,* Frederic Remington's watercolor *Harnessing the Mules,* and a hallway frieze created by his friend Ed Borein. Borein was one of the most prolific Western artists. The Bradford Brinton Memorial collection holds more than 175 pieces by this master.

Among the memorial's distinguished visitors have been Queen Elizabeth II, Prince Philip, and James Michener. Many Western historians visit the Brinton art and artifact collection each year.

Brinton died in 1936 and left the house and ranch to his sister, Helen. Her will created the Bradford Brinton Memorial which opened in 1961. Each year a different art exhibit is featured in the gallery. The memorial is open daily from 9:30 A.M. to 5:00 P.M. May 15 through Labor Day. Each year the memorial sponsors a special Christmas holiday art exhibit featuring a single artist. For information on regular and special exhibits call 672–3173.

◆ **Spahn's Big Horn Bed & Breakfast** is 6 miles beyond Big Horn on Highway 335. Drive till the pavement ends, then proceed another half mile on the gravel road to the Spahns' sign. Turn left and follow the road up into the trees and hills for ¾ mile. Ron and Bobbie Spahn built the log home from scratch using little modern equipment, and the result is a beautiful home and bed and breakfast with a gorgeous view of the valley and surrounding mountains. Ron groomed a number of cross-country skiing and hiking trails through the woods, where rabbits and deer will pleasantly surprise you. For kids of all ages and sizes, there are lambs to pet in the barn area.

We spent an anniversary weekend there and enjoyed the breeze blowing through the whispering pines and the snow softly falling outside our window. Your hosts know the area well and can direct you to any number of attractions and roads to travel for beautiful scenery. Rates range from $60 to $100 a night depending on accommodations and season. For information and reservations call 674–8150.

Return to Highway 87 through Big Horn and head south to a region filled with history and remnants of the Indian Wars. The first site you come upon is about 13 miles down the road. Massacre Hill marks the site of the Fetterman Fight of 1866. The 20-foot high impressive rock ◆ **Fetterman Massacre Monument** sits on top of the hill, overlooking the battlefield. Captain William J. Fetterman, who cut his teeth during the Civil War, knew little about the strategy of fighting Indians.

The skirmish resulted from the government's construction of Fort Phil Kearny in direct violation of the U.S. treaty with the Sioux Nation. Led by Red Cloud and Crazy Horse, a band of Arapahoe, Cheyenne, and Sioux Indians retaliated on December 21, 1866, by ambushing Captain Fetterman and his troops, who had been sent to rescue a wagon train under attack. More than eighty soldiers and civilians were killed during the battle. There were no survivors. Evidence indicates that Captain Fetterman and one of his officers chose to perish by their own hands. The Indians called this fight the "battle of one-hundred-in-the-hands." The shooting started about noon and ended about a half hour later. The massacre created fear that the Indians would then attack Fort Phil Kearny and sent John "Portugee" Phillips on his 236-mile blizzard-hampered ride to seek reinforcements from Fort Laramie. Phillips' horse collapsed and died when he arrived at Fort Laramie on Christmas night. Despite outnumbering the soldiers at Fort Phil Kearny by several thousand to just over a hundred, the Indians never attacked. Reinforcements arrived two weeks later. A number of interpretive plaques at the battlefield bring the bloody scene back to life and discuss the fateful decisions Fetterman made during the conflict. Like Custer, Fetterman imprudently ignored the rules of Indian fighting and plunged his outnumbered troops into history with their final battle. It was the worst loss suffered by the army in western battles until Custer's Last Stand, not far away at Little Big Horn nearly ten years later.

The next August, Indians again staged an attack, this time on a detail of twenty-eight soldiers and four civilians on a woodcutting mission under the command of Captian James Powell. The ◆ **Wagon Box Fight** got its name because soldiers defended themselves from attack for more than three hours by removing the wheels from their wagons and arranging the fourteen wagon boxes into a circular protective barricade. The improvised fort, combined with the soldiers' newly-issued and innovative Springfield breech-loading rifles, which could fire up to twenty rounds per minute, turned the tide against the Indians even though they far outnumbered the soldiers. Three white men were killed and two wounded. Indian casualty estimates ranged from a dozen to in excess of a thousand. A relief force from Fort Phil Kearny chased off the remaining Indians. The Wagon Box Monument is located near Story. Directional signs easily lead you to the battle site.

JOHNSON COUNTY

The bloodiest Indian battles took place at and around ◆ **Fort Phil Kearny.** We have already toured the Fetterman Massacre and Wagon Box Fight historical sites in Sheridan County. Now we turn to Fort Phil Kearny itself. The fort was established in July

1866 as a command post for the 18th Infantry to protect the Bozeman Trail. It was named after a popular Union general killed in the Civil War. Constructed from logs cut in and hauled from the Big Horn Mountains, the post was one of the few palisade fortifications in the West. More than four thousand logs were used to erect the stockade.

After the Union Pacific Railroad laid its tracks far enough west that travelers could avoid the Bozeman Trail, the forts protecting the Bozeman Trail were no longer necessary. General Ulysses S. Grant ordered the closing of Fort Phil Kearny after the Treaty of 1868. Shortly thereafter, Indians burned the abandoned fort to the ground. As a result of the Treaty, the area belonged exclusively to the Indians until the conclusion of the Indian Wars in 1877.

The Fort Phil Kearny Museum and Visitors Center is open April 1 through May 14 and October 1 through November 30 from noon to 4:00 P.M. on Wednesday through Sunday. From May 15 to September 30, it's open from 8:00 A.M. to 6:00 P.M. daily. It is closed December through March. There is a $1.00 gate fee. The fort grounds are open year-round from dawn to dusk. Bozeman Trail Days in mid-June are headquartered at the fort. Activities include both white and Native American interpretations of the Wagon Box Fight and Fetterman Massacre, archaeological tours, and living-history programs. There are a number of historic interpretive signs and markers at the fort. Fort Phil Kearny is located at exit 44 off Interstate 90. From Story take Highway 193 southeast about 5 miles to the road leading to the post. For information call 684–7629.

Father Pierre Jean DeSmet (named "Black Robe" by the Indians) left his mark on Wyoming as the first Catholic missionary. He passed Independence Rock and celebrated the first Roman Catholic mass in the territory near Daniel in 1840. He also discovered **Lake DeSmet** in 1851. At the time, it was the second largest salt lake in the West, behind the Great Salt Lake. Lake DeSmet is located 8 miles northeast of Buffalo off Highway 87. Ask the locals about the dragon of Lake DeSmet, which devours young maidens. There's also an 18-foot high Father DeSmet Monument overlooking the lake at a turnout along Highway 87. You can take advantage of the picnic and camping sites around the lake.

Johnson County was not only the scene of some of the most vicious fighting between whites and Indians in the West, it also gave birth to the 1892 Johnson County War of owners of large ranches against homesteaders (also called nesters) and smaller ranchers. Cattle were rustled and homesteads were burned.

The absentee cattle barons from Cheyenne put out the word in Texas that they were seeking gunslingers at $5.00 per day and a $50 bonus for every man killed in Johnson County. On April 6, 1892, a train carrying twenty-six hired guns from Texas and another couple dozen Wyoming men departed from Cheyenne. They were headed by Major Frank Wolcott, a former Union army officer now in the employ of the Wyoming Stock Growers Association, which was ruled by the large cattle outfits.

Carrying a "dead list" of seventy known and suspected rustlers and sympathizers (including Johnson County sheriff Red Angus), the "Invaders" first stopped at the KC Ranch near present day Kaycee and ambushed two men on their list, Nick Ray and Nate Champion. The battle went on for hours. Ray died early in the battle and Champion fought until the gunmen torched the cabin and shot him as he fled the flames. Wolcott and his army then moved 30 miles north to the TA Ranch, where they holed up and awaited the arrival of Sheriff Angus. An informer had told them that Angus had gathered an armed force and was moving in their direction. At daylight, the Cheyenne Invaders found themselves surrounded by two hundred well-armed and enraged Buffalo-area ranchers and nesters. A running three-day gun battle cost two of the Texas men their lives. Peace was finally restored after Wyoming governor Barber cabled President Harrison for federal assistance. The president sent troops from nearby Fort McKinney to quell the uprising. The cavalry arrived as Sheriff Angus and his "Defenders" prepared to attack the house with dynamite as they approached behind a contraption fashioned from two wagons lashed together. The rescuing cavalry escorted the invading gunmen and their leaders to Fort McKinley and later returned them to Cheyenne. None of the perpetrators were ever prosecuted. The men were let go on the pretense that Johnson County could not afford to pay for the trial. Although the cattle barons' hired guns got off without so much as a day in jail, the Johnson County War marked the end of the iron reign of the big cattle barons.

Look for the **Johnson County Cattle War Commemorative Bronzes** on Buffalo's South Main Street near the intersection of Angus Street. The three-quarters life-size sculptures by artist D. Michael Thomas, *Ridin' for the Brand* and *Living on the Edge,* depict the deadly face-offs between the cattle barons' men and small ranchers and just plain rustlers.

The Johnson County War display in the ◆**Jim Gatchell Museum of the West** at the corner of Main and Fort Streets in Buffalo also gives a detailed description of the times and events leading up to and including the cattle war. A ring belonging to slain Nate Champion is among the cattle war memorabilia. The museum's Native American artifact collection is one of the largest in Wyoming. Particularly interesting are the Cattle War, Wagon Box Fight, and 1880s Buffalo Main Street dioramas. Bugler Adolph Metzger's crushed bugle testifies to the final moments of the Fetterman Massacre. Pioneer druggist Jim Gatchell's Western and Native American collections form the nucleus of the museum's holdings. The museum is located in the 1909 Carnegie Library Building, not to be overlooked. Check out its interesting Neoclassical architectural features. The museum is open during May, September, and October on Monday through Friday 9:00 A.M. to 5:00 P.M. and June through August daily (except July 4) 9:00 A.M. to 8:00 P.M. It is closed October through April.

Buffalo (population 3,358) has a historic Main Street that's worth a few hours of browsing. Ask for a self-guided Main Street Walking Tour brochure at the chamber of commerce at 55 North Main Street. Many of the buildings have historic pictures in their front windows or on mounted plaques. The tour includes more than twenty buildings. For information call 684–5544 or (800) 277–5122.

A good place to start your tour is at the old **Occidental Hotel,** made famous in Owen Wister's novel *The Virginian.* Located at 10 North Main Street, the hotel no longer has rooms to let but is on the National Register of Historic Places. In the beginning the 1880 hotel was a log structure, which was replaced in 1910 by the current brick building. At one time the hotel occupied the whole block. Today, various businesses operate out of the the block-long structure. For example, a barbershop operates in the original barbershop location, with the barber chairs from the first shop. **Deerfield at the Occidental Saloon,** a neat women's boutique and espresso bar, resides in the hotel's former saloon and still has the 1910 tin ceiling and back bar with a stained-glass canopy. Ask to see the bullet hole in the bar drawer. There's also a 1944 wall mural of the Hole in the Wall, the famous canyon area where Butch Cassidy's gang hung out, painted by a down-and-out saloon customer to pay off his bar tab.

At Two North Main Street try out the **Busy Bee Lunch.** The site started out as a popcorn stand, but the Busy Bee has been here since 1928. It's a regular spot for the locals, and the homemade pies are mouthwatering. Don't look for any tables—it's strictly a stools and counter kind of place. You can eat your pie as you watch and listen to Clear Creek flowing by right outside the window.

After your pie, stroll down to **Seney's Drugs** at 38 South Main Street and belly up to the bar or at least up to the soda fountain, which has been a favorite Buffalo gathering spot for generations. Seney's malted milks and milk shakes were recommended by Duncan Hines in his newspaper column. The 1895 building at 84–89 South Main Street features a white cast-iron facade on the second floor.

Look at the mural on the side of the building at 51 South Main Street. It proclaims Buffalo as more than a "One Horse Town." A variety of businesses have operated out of the structure through the decades, including a butcher shop, grocery store, barbershop, jewelry store, and city electric building. Today, the **Hitching Post Art Gallery** represents the work of state and local artists with a fine array of unique wildlife and Western limited editions, woodcarvings, pottery, baskets, beadwork, sterling silver jewelry, and bronzes. For information call 684–9473.

Spend an hour or two at **Buffalo's Washington Park** pitching horseshoes, taking a hike, picnicking, or cooling off in Wyoming's largest free outdoor swimming pool. The park is located at the intersection of Burritt Avenue and Angus Street. Clear Creek flows through the park and you can avail yourself of Clear Creek Trail System, which traverses the park, downtown historic district, and wildlife areas.

Also located on Burritt Avenue, at 590 North Burritt, is the ◆ **Cloud Peak Inn,** a bed-and-breakfast establishment in a grand turn-of the-century house, once the "in town" home of a wealthy rancher. Luxurious oak paneling, a fossil fireplace, and plentiful gourmet cooking are some of the attractions. Unwind on the porch, on the balcony, or in the Jacuzzi. Prices are in the $50 to $100 per night range. For information or reservations call 684–5794.

A number of day trips out of Buffalo provide a range of activities and sights. Pick up a copy of the "Scenic Tours of Johnson County" brochure at the chamber of commerce for a complete listing and description, but here are a few of our favorites for your consideration. Start with a half-day tour of ❖ **Crazy Woman Canyon** on Highway 16 headed directly west toward the Big Horn Mountains. Crazy Woman Canyon Road is well signed and branches off to the left about 25 miles out of town. This is mountain terrain, so make sure your brakes are good before starting out. It's also not a place where you will want to tow a trailer. You'll drive through the ancient canyon and view dramatic cliffs and gigantic boulders that have tumbled down the canyon walls. A Sioux legend says the creek was the haunt of an old insane squaw who could be seen shooting the rapids in her canoe and leaping from village to village like a spirit on moonlit nights. Other legends offer different explanations for the name of the canyon and creek. To return to Buffalo, continue along the gravel road that took you through the canyon, until you reach Highway 196. Turn left and you'll be back in town in 10 miles.

You can also go on a several-hour trip that takes you back millions of years to see the **Dry Creek Petrified Tree.** Proceed east on Interstate 90 until the Red Hills exit. Take the gravel road north for 5 miles and then turn left and follow that road to the petrified tree and stumps. The self-guided tour includes a series of eight informative ecological stations. The petrified trees were cypress trees and lived in a climate similar to that of Georgia's Okefenokee Swamp.

Meet up with Butch Cassidy at the ❖ **Outlaw Cave,** a full day's journey. The cave is located on public land with access via Bureau of Land Management roads. First, drive south to Kaycee on Interstate 25 and then head about .9 mile west on Highway 190 to the Barnum Road junction. Follow Barnum Road 17 miles to a sign for the Middle Fork Management Area of the Powder River. Take a left at this sign onto the gravel-and-dirt road designated as the Bar C Road. Most of the road is hard surfaced in dry weather; however, the upper portion requires a vehicle with high clearance, and preferably four-wheel drive, or you can hike the final section of the trip. After traveling 8½ miles from the Middle Fork sign, you will encounter the Outlaw Cave turnoff. From this point, it's approximately 2 miles to the cave. The scenery is captivating, with beautiful panoramas of red mountain walls and a cascading river. You're also within walking distance of the **Indian Rock Art Cave,** which has seventeen carvings including one of a large warrior figure. The infamous Hole in the Wall is located nearby on private property.

A more adventuresome way to see the Hole in the Wall country is on horseback. Contact **Country Tours** in Kaycee for information on their guided seven-to-eight-hour tours to the Hole in the Wall and the Bloody Bozeman Trail. For information call 738–2243 or inquire at the Kaycee Texaco Station.

The Hole in the Wall Gang, headed by Butch Cassidy (Robert Leroy Parker), and the Sundance Kid (Harry Longabaugh) often hid out in the territory around Kaycee after their evildoings such as robbing trains and banks. You can see the Hole in the Wall cabin used by Butch Cassidy and his cohorts at the Old Trail Town in Cody.

Before you leave the Kaycee area, you'll want to read the KILLING OF CHAMPION AND RAY informative sign detailing the Johnson County Cattle War battle at the TA Ranch. The marker is located just south of Kaycee on the east side of old Highway 89.

WASHAKIE COUNTY

Leaving Buffalo via Highway 16 west puts you on another part of the **Big Horn Scenic Byways.** The road climbs up out of Buffalo into some wonderful mountain country crossing over the Big Horns through the Powder River Pass at an elevation of 9,666 feet. There are ample campgrounds and recreation areas if you want to spend a day or two in the wilderness. Ten Sleep Canyon has sheer red-and-buff-colored limestone cliffs, and Ten Sleep Creek offers good trout fishing. As on Highway 14, you'll see breathtaking mountains, canyons, rivers, and wildflowers, plus abundant wildlife.

The name of the town of Ten Sleep (population 330) comes from the Sioux Indians, who had a large camp along the North Platte River near Casper. They measured distance by the number of days or "sleeps" it took to get somewhere. It was ten sleeps from the North Platte River camp to the present-day site of Ten Sleep, a crossroads to other camps and hunting areas.

Ten Sleep Pioneer Museum is located on the east edge of town in the Ten Sleep Public Park, a nice place for a picnic. The museum includes history and memorabilia from the Spring Creek Raid. Battles between cattlemen and sheep ranchers in the

West were legend. To preserve "their" range, cattlemen set up boundaries, or "deadlines" (so-called because if sheep crossed the line they and their owners could soon be dead), beyond which sheep were forbidden.

In late March 1909, a French sheepman named Joe Allemand with his nephew Jules Lazier and Joe Emge, a cattleman turned sheepman, left Worland with 5,000 sheep and headed toward Spring Creek, southeast of Ten Sleep. On April 2, 1909, seven masked men raided the sheepherders' camp, killing all three men and a number of sheep. Five of the raiders were sent to prison for their deed while the other two plea-bargained. The killings created a public uproar and virtually ended the range war between cattlemen and sheepmen. A monument marks the site of the tragedy. It's on the east side of Highway 434 about 6½ miles southeast of Ten Sleep. The museum is open Memorial Day through Labor Day from noon to 6:00 P.M. The address is 500 Second Street.

As you drive west on Highway 16 from Ten Sleep, you'll pass magnificent red cliffs above the Norwood River. Native Americans used the tops of these cliffs to send signals to the Greybull area, 50 miles northwest as the crow flies.

The Big Horn Basin on the western side of the Big Horn Mountains has rich land, a longer-than-average growing season, and warmer temperatures. Worland (population 5,742) is situated right on the banks of the Big Horn River and is principally an agricultural community, with the Holly Sugar plant providing a strong base for the area's economy.

The town was founded in 1903 (late for Wyoming) and named after one of the first pioneers to homestead in the area. Charlie "Dad" Worland ran a makeshift saloon and stage station, and A. G. Rupp built a general store in the early days. In 1906 the Chicago, Burlington and Quincy Railroad arrived, and a year later the more than 50-mile Big Horn Irrigation Canal was constructed, making Worland a growing agricultural and trade center.

Peter Toth chose Worland as the Wyoming location for his ◆ *Trail of the Whispering Giants* monument. Toth spent nearly two decades traveling the country and carving towering wooden Native American sculptures in each of the fifty states. He finished the Worland statue in September 1980. The massive carvings were a gift to each state; Toth accepted no payments.

105

The only requirements to receive a statue were the donation of a permanent pedestal and a commitment to maintain the statue. The Hungarian refugee began his unusual quest in February 1972 in La Jolla, California, where he built his first Indian monument, and finished his final sculpture in May 1988 in Haleiwa, Hawaii. The Wyoming *Trail of the Whispering Giants* monument sits majestically on the southwest corner of the Washakie County Courthouse lawn.

Washakie County Museum and Cultural Center operates out of an old Latter-day Saints church at 1115 Obie Sue Avenue. Inside, you will find a recreation of the A. G. Rupp General Store, Soapy Dale Peak Lodge (a Shoshone Sheepeater mountain shelter), and an exhibit of early 1900s black-and-white photographs by Rico Stine, showing the town and surrounding area. The museum sponsors an annual symposium in July for paleontologists working in the Big Horn Mountains. The museum is open May through October on Monday through Friday from 10:00 A.M. to 5:00 P.M. and Sundays from 2:00 to 4:00 P.M. During the rest of the year, hours are Monday through Friday 10:00 A.M. to 4:00 P.M. For information call 347–4102.

Antone's Supper Club (347–2301), 3 miles east of town on Highway 16, and the dining room of the Deer Haven Lodge (366–2449), 7 miles east on Highway 16, are popular eating places.

Less than 3 miles north of Worland on Highway 433 marks **Jim Bridger Historic Trail.** Frequent conflicts with Native Americans along the Bozeman Trail created the need for an alternative route to the western Montana goldfields in the 1860s. Scout and explorer Jim Bridger blazed a new trail for the miners across the Big Horn Basin near present-day Worland.

HOT SPRINGS COUNTY

Both Hot Springs County and Thermopolis (population 3,247) got their names from the world's largest natural hot springs, located at Thermopolis. The Thermopolis anticline (a geological fold with rock strata sloping downward on both sides of a common crest) is the largest of several folds along the southern shoulder of the Big Horn Basin. Fractured rock within the anticline permits an avenue of rainwater and snowmelt to seep down into the hotter rocks underground before rising again to the surface as hot springs.

The summer drive into ◆ **Hot Springs State Park** is inviting, with beautiful flower gardens lining the way. The entrance is adorned with a large calcified monolith called Tepee Fountain. An 1896 treaty signed by Shoshone chief Washakie and Arapahoe chief Sharp Nose gave the healing waters of the hot springs to the white man with the condition that their people always have free access to a portion of the hot springs. Thus, the State Bath House is open to everyone at no charge. If you don't bring your own towel or swimsuit, they will be furnished for a small fee.

Sink your body into the soothing hot mineral waters, kept at a temperature of 104 degrees Fahrenheit. Facilities include private lockers, showers and both an inside and outside hot mineral pool. You can enjoy the majestic bluffs while you let the minerals and heat relax your body. The bathhouse hours are Monday through Saturday from 8:00 A.M. to 5:30 P.M. and on Sundays from noon to 5:30 P.M. It is closed on holidays during the winter but open on holidays during the summer, noon to 5:30 P.M. The park is located at 220 Park Street. For information call 864–3765.

Privately-owned hot springs facilities offer a bit more for the kids, such as water slides, large outdoor swimming pools, saunas, Jacuzzis and game arcades. The Star Plunge is open daily from 9:00 A.M. to 9:00 P.M. except December 1–20. An all-day pass costs around $6.00. For information call 864–3771. The Hot Springs Water Park offers similar facilities and prices and can be reached at 864–9250.

Don't miss the other park activites, such as taking a walk across the replica of a 1916 swinging bridge, which spans the Big Horn River and offers a great view of Mineral Terrace; using the picnic facilities; or riding along Buffalo Pasture Road to get a look at the central buffalo herd for the Wyoming state parks. For a map of the buffalo grazing areas, pick up a Hot Springs Park brochure at the headquarters near the entrance to the park.

Every summer in early August the Hot Springs State Park, in conjunction with local Native Americans, puts on the **Gift of the Waters Pageant** commemorating the signing of the treaty, transferring of the hot springs, and Legend of Bah-gue-wana. The hot springs were known to the Indians as *Bah-gue-wana* or "Smoking Waters." The pageant is an excellent opportunity to see Indians in the full splendor of their ceremonial clothing, experience their dances, and learn about tribal legends. For information on the pageant call the Thermopolis Chamber of Commerce at 864–3192.

A new Thermopolis attraction with ties to ancient history is **The Wyoming Dinosaur Center.** Follow the green dinosaur tracks painted on the streets to the dinosaur museum. Visitors will see dinosaur-bone preparation in the laboratory and at excavation locations. The 16,000-square-foot center is dedicated to keeping Wyoming's dinosaurs in Wyoming. For now, the main room showcases full-scale casts of a stegosaur and sauropod from China as well as other fossils. Since the early 1990s, paleontologist Ed Cole has made a number of discoveries in the mountains east of Thermopolis, one of which promises to be one of the largest dinosaur finds in the Rocky Mountains. Fees are $5.00 for the museum and $15.00 for a tour of the dinosaur excavation site. Hours are 8:00 A.M. to 7:00 P.M. Monday through Saturday, and 10:00 A.M. to 7:00 P.M. on Sunday May 1 through June 30 and September 1 through October 31. The hours from July 1 through August 31 are Monday through Saturday 8:00 A.M. to 10:00 P.M. and Sunday 10:00 A.M. to 7:00 P.M. During the rest of year, the museum can be visited by special appointment. For information call 864–2997.

The **Hot Springs Historical Museum,** at 700 Broadway, has rightfully earned its reputation as one of the best museums in the nation. Among its exhibits of Western and local history are stagecoaches, the historic cherry-wood bar from the Hole in the Wall Saloon frequented by Butch Cassidy, a display on the coal industry, Native American artifacts, and a frontier town complete with newspaper office, dentist's office, and general store. The $1.00–$2.00 entrance fee is well worth it. The museum is open year-round Tuesday through Saturday from 8:00 A.M. to 5:00 P.M. except for Thanksgiving, Christmas, and New Year's Day. For information call 864–5183.

For winter travelers, Thermopolis sponsors **Cutting Horse Competitions** November through March. For information on these horse-drawn sleigh races, call 864–2466 or 864–3401.

Pumpernick's, at 512 Broadway, serves great muffins, sandwiches, and dinners in a cozy atmosphere. Prices are inexpensive to moderate. For information call 864–5151.

A. J. and Marina Dilley have done a tremendous job completely restoring the old landmark hotel in Thermopolis. Today it's a delightful place known as the ❖ **Broadway Inn Bed & Breakfast,** located in the heart of Thermopolis at 342 Broadway. Enjoy your delicious multicourse breakfast—complete with buffalo sausage if you wish—in a cheerful front sunroom, or relax in the French Victorian lobby area. Marina, who was born in Holland, has decorated the inn with an international touch. Each of the four guest rooms and two suites has its own distinctive decor and private bath. Choose from lace to rustic Western. An old-fashioned claw-foot tub makes for a great soak. Rates are in the $50–$100 range per night and include a full breakfast. For information or reservations call 864–2636.

Around Thermopolis, the country provides a variety of sightseeing options. A drive through the ❖ **Wind River Canyon** presents vistas not equaled anywhere else. You ride next to towering cliffs while beside you the raging Big Horn River churns white. The canyon also exhibits one of the best exposed and complete cross-sections of geologic time in central Wyoming. As you make your way through the canyon you will pass rocks covering the breadth of geologic time from sixty-six-million-year-old Cretaceous formations to Precambrian layers more than two billion years old. There are a number of turnouts for fantastic photo ops and picnicking. Be sure to look at the precarious train track on the opposite side of the canyon. In 1995 a large rock slide obliterated sections of the track. The Chicago, Burlington and Quincy Railroad first went through the canyon in 1911, followed by the state highway in 1925. It's approximately a 60-mile round-trip from Thermopolis to Boysen State Park (see page 67) on Highway 20.

If you want to experience the Wind River close up, consider a trip with **Wind River Canyon Whitewater,** operating out of Thermopolis at 907 Shoshone. The season runs approximately from Memorial Day to Labor Day. For information call 864–9343, or 486–2253 during the off-season.

Outlaw Trail, Inc., a nonprofit community group of Thermopolis, organizes a once-a-year 100-mile trail ride for one hundred riders. Reservations are on a first-come, first-served basis. The trip caters to experienced riders since each rider must care for his or her own horse and tack. You'll follow the Outlaw Trail of Butch Cassidy and other desperados and hear yarns around the campfire or maybe weave some tall ones of your own. For information call 864–2287 or write Outlaw Trail, Inc., Box 1046, Thermopolis 82443.

Some of Wyoming's most interesting petroglyphs lie within an hour's drive of Thermopolis. For directions and the keys to the gate at the ❖ **Legend Rock Petroglyph Site** contact the Hot Springs State Park Headquarters on Park Street in Thermopolis or call 864–2176. Legend Rock contains hundreds of yards of sandstone cliffs covered with dozens of unique petroglyphs. The oldest works date back two thousand years. You can drive to within a hundred yards of the cliff face. The site facilities include a summer rest room and picnic tables. To get to Legend Rock, take Highway 120 northwest toward Meeteetse. About 21 miles out of Thermopolis, turn left on the Hamilton Dome Road; there's a large sign for the High Island Ranch & Cattle Company here. Drive 5 miles west on the paved road and then turn right at the fork in the road onto Cottonwood Creek Road. The road to the petroglyph site is immediately to the left after the second cattle guard.

Our favorite petroglyph is the rabbit with big ears. It is drawn in the style of figures painted by the New Mexico Mimbres culture during A.D. 900–1000. It is the only known rabbit rock art in Wyoming. Other intriguing figures include *kokopelli*, an insect or hump-backed flute player. It's an old symbol representing fertility and demonstrating linkages between ancient North and South American peoples. The bird petroglyph is very common in Wyoming rock art and is typically termed the "Ghost Dance Style Bird."

An Arapahoe elder, Paul Moss, calls the turtle petroglyph the "Creation Panel." In Arapahoe legend the turtle dove down to the bottom of the ocean and brought up the mud on his back and formed the continents. In Native American teaching, the turtle represents the oldest symbol for the earth. Please refrain from touching the petroglyphs, so they can be preserved for the pleasure and education of future generations.

You are now within a few miles of a unique working cattle ranch. After exiting from the petroglyph road, take a left on Cottonwood Creek Road and follow it 3 miles until you see a large sheep wagon and a road leading off to the left. The ❖ **High Island Ranch & Cattle Company** consists of a lower lodge at

6,000 feet on the high plains and an upper lodge in the Owl Creek Mountains at an elevation of 9,000 feet. Overall, there are forty-five thousand acres to investigate. About 35 miles from the main camp, the mountain lodge at Rock Creek offers excellent trout fishing within a stone's throw of the front porch. As you ride from the rangeland of the prairie into the Owl Creek Mountains, you will experience the never-to-be-forgotten sights of the Washakie Needles, a 75-foot-high waterfall, majestic elk, and ancient tipi rings.

Riding activities include a real honest-to-goodness 1800s-period cattle drive in late August, cattle roundup weeks throughout the summer, and individual riding experiences. You'll become part of the 1800s as authentic mountain men join you around the campfire. Get ready for high adventure as you move those dogies and then sleep under the stars to a coyote serenade. Back at the ranch, you'll feast on barbecue, and enjoy a western hoedown and other entertainment to wind up the week. Frank and Karen Robbins run a class act, delivering a week that is sure to change your life. The staff take pride in their way of life and are more than eager to share the western experience with you. Whether you choose to relax or work the ranch from pre-sunup to sundown, pick your week and sit in the saddle. You'll need to bring an assortment of gear to participate in the trail rides (call for information). Weekly rates run from $1,000 to $1,500. For information and reservations call 867–2374. The regular ranch season runs from mid-May through mid-September. If hunting is more your game, inquire about the ranch's hunting season, which takes place September through November.

BIG HORN COUNTY

From High Island Ranch take Highway 120 north to Highway 431 east for a 30-mile scenic backcountry drive and then travel north 28 miles on Highway 433 along the picturesque Big Horn River to reach Big Horn County. Turn right on to Highway 31 at Manderson (population 83) for a visit to the ◆ **Medicine Lodge State Archaeological Site.** Located 6 miles northeast of Hyattville off Cold Springs Road, the archaeological site is one of the most significant in the United States. Medicine Lodge

111

Creek runs through the lush meadows and thick groves of trees, offering excellent picnicking and fishing opportunities. The site's plentiful food, shelter, and water have attracted people for more than 10,000 years.

The diggings have been filled in for preservation purposes, but prehistoric petroglyphs and pictographs remain on the red sandstone cliffs, and interpretive material at the cliffs and in the log cabin visitors center provides a glimpse of the sixty cultures that once camped at the site. Surrounding the site is the 12,100-acre Medicine Lodge Wildlife Habitat Management Area, a refuge for an extensive elk herd and numerous other types of wildlife. A self-guided brochure leads you to different petroglyphs along the cliff walls. The Medicine Lodge State Archaeological Site is open from May 1 through November 4, and the visitors center is open from May 1 to Labor Day. For information call 469–2234.

There's a wonderful backcountry scenic byway that brings you out around Shell and is worth taking if you have a four-wheel-drive vehicle. Inquire about road conditions and directions at the archaeological site visitors center. The Shell Stone Schoolhouse is listed on the National Register of Historic Places. It was built in 1903 and was the first non-log community building in the area. It was in use until the early 1950s. From Shell head east for another tour of the **Big Horn Scenic Byway** through Shell Canyon's gorge, with its incredible falls, on Highway 14. Be on the lookout for the statuesque red Chimney Rock near the west entrance to Shell Canyon. You will travel briefly into Sheridan County but a left at Burgess Junction onto Highway 14A west will get you back into Big Horn County.

A highly sacred Native American location, ◆ **Medicine Wheel** is also a National Historic Landmark. Native Americans periodically perform religious ceremonies here. Located at the top of Medicine Mountain at an elevation of nearly 10,000 feet, the wheel consists of twenty-eight spokes radiating out from a central hub. The hub and spokes are 80 feet in diameter and are made from unhewed rock pieces. There are six other mounds, or cairns, spaced unevenly around the rim. Each mound has an opening facing a different direction, and the wheel rim has a break in its eastern edge.

The origin and meaning of the wheel are still debated. Some scientists believe it resembles the Mexican calendar stone, while others believe it was used for other astrological purposes. In any event, observing the Medicine Wheel is a powerful and mysterious experience. Although they had no direct connection to the Medicine Wheel, Chief Joseph of the Nez Perce fasted at the site and Shoshone chief Washakie visited the spot to seek guidance in leading his nation. Native Americans have traditionally traveled to mountain peaks for prayer, seeking spiritual harmony with the powerful spirits there. Please respect the worship of Native Americans during your visit and do not disturb any of the cultural artifacts.

The Medicine Wheel National Historic Landmark is administered by the U.S. Forest Service. The site provides breathtaking vistas of the Big Horn Basin, Wind River, and the Absaroka and Pryor ranges. The Medicine Wheel is located off Highway 14A 3 miles north on Forest Service Road 12. It is about 30 miles west of Burgess Junction and 27 miles east of Lovell. Vehicles pulling trailers are not recommended on the narrow dirt road leading to the parking area. There is a 1½-mile walk from the parking area to the Medicine Wheel. For information call 548–6541.

Surrounded by mountains on three sides—the spectacular Absaroka and Beartooth ranges to the west, the rugged Pryor Mountains to the north, and the playground of the Big Horns to the east—Lovell (population 2,131) grew out of the area's largest ranch. The ML Ranch, founded by Anthony L. Mason and Henry Clay Lovell in 1880, managed twenty-five thousand head of cattle. The town of Lovell began in 1890 and incorporated in 1906, with ranching and the sugar industry providing economic stability.

Lovell is known as the Rose City of Wyoming, with beautiful planters and gardens of roses gracing the streets, parks, and private yards. The 120,000-acre ◆ **Bighorn Canyon National Recreation Area** combines a variety of majestic scenery, from badlands to canyons with magnificent gorges to high prairie trails. The Yellowtail Dam in Montana, dedicated in 1968, created 71-mile-long Bighorn Lake, a prime recreational and camping area. Stop at the solar-heated National Park Bighorn Canyon Visitor Center at the east edge of Lovell for maps of the area and directions to various attractions. The visitor center also shows an orientation film on Bighorn Canyon's history, natural features, and available activities. For information call 548–2251.

At the historic Mason-Lovell (ML) Ranch you can visit the bunkhouse, blacksmith shop, and the married ranch hands' cabin. North on Highway 37 you'll discover the nation's first wild horse preserve in the 47,000-acre **Pryor Mountain Wild Horse Range.** The mustangs possess the distinctive dun color and dorsal and zebra stripes typical of horses with Spanish ancestry. These features are not common in wild horse bands. You can, if you'd like, adopt a horse through the Bureau of Land Management's wild horse management program.

To view the spectacular cliffs of Bighorn Canyon from another vantage point, take a trip up the canyon with the *Canyon Queen* **Tourboat.** For information and rates call 548–7230.

A short loop tour out of Lovell takes you through the towns of Byron, Deaver, Frannie, and Cowley, with a combined population under 1,300. Five miles east of Lovell on Highway 14A, there's an informative marker on the 37-mile **Sidon Irrigation Canal,** completed by the Mormons in 1895. Work on the project was halted by a large boulder that was in the way. According to legend, prayer and divine intervention caused the rock to split, allowing the canal work to proceed. The split rock became known as Prayer Rock. Three miles east is the oilfield community of Byron, with a number of old log structures. This area has produced more than 117 million barrels of oil and 13 million cubic feet of gas since 1918.

Taking Highway 114 north, you next arrive at Deaver and the **Deaver Reservoir,** which is teeming with bluegills and crappies. Six miles north on Highway 310/789 and just 2 miles south of the Montana state line is Frannie (population 148), "The Biggest Little Town in Wyoming." You can stand in the middle of Frannie and have one foot in Big Horn County and the other foot in Park County. The town of Cowley, several miles east of Deaver, sports a host of historic sandstone buildings worthy of a look. It's also home to a number of artesian wells with 98 percent pure water. Stop for a refreshing sip before heading back to Lovell.

Follow Highway 310/789 south 30 miles to Greybull (population 1,789), home to some of the world's finest dinosaur beds and located at the confluence of the Big Horn and Greybull rivers and Shell and Dry creeks. The town was established in 1909 as a stop along the Chicago Burlington and Quincy Railroad and derives its name from the legendary albino bison sacred to

Native Americans. One of the world's largest Allosauruses ("Big Al") was excavated near here, and since 1934 paleontologists have unearthed twelve large sauropods. The dinosaur beds are located 10 miles north of Shell on Bureau of Land Management property and are open to the public.

Sheep Mountain, a 15-mile-long ridge 1,000 feet high, rises to the northeast of Greybull. It's a perfect example of a doubly plunging anticline. Red Devil signs lead you to Devil's Kitchen, where fossil and rock finds are common. Ask for directions at the Greybull Chamber of Commerce on Highway 16, or call 765–2100.

Fossils, petrified wood, Native American relics, and semiprecious stones form the nucleus of the excellent **Greybull Museum** at 325 Greybull Avenue. The museum is open daily except Sunday, June 1 through Labor Day from 10:00 A.M. to 8:00 P.M.; Labor Day to November 1 from 2:00 to 5:00 P.M.; and the rest of the year from 2:00 to 4:00 P.M. For information call 765–2444.

At the Greybull Airport, examples of World War II's mighty bombers and transport aircraft make up the ✦**Museum of Flight and Aerial Firefighting.** You'll learn that the first aerial fire reconnaissance took place in 1919 in California. Before the advent of the radio, messages were relayed to ground via notes dropped by parachute or transported by carrier pigeon. You'll also see five of the remaining flying P84Y-2s used against the Japanese in the South Pacific theater during World War II.

Follow the Greybull River west toward Meeteetse, first on Greybull River Road and then south on Highway 30. You'll pop out of the sagebrush countryside 7 miles north of Meeteetse.

PARK COUNTY

Sporting a population of only 368, Meeteetse offers a variety of interesting sites. The name derives from the Crow Indian word for "meeting place of the chiefs." Stop in at the more than 100-year-old **Cowboy Bar** at 1936 State Street for a sarsaparilla. Take a gander at the hand-carved Italian rose and cherry-wood bar. The Meeteetse Social Club meets regularly at the saloon on the weekend for an old-fashioned gathering with card playing and socializing. The telephone number is 868–2585. Wander next door to the nearly 100-year-old **Meeteetse Mercantile Company** to catch the flavor of an Old West general store. It stocks a wide array of products, from yard goods to home furnishings. For the tourist, there's a good selection of books on the West and on Western clothing. The address is 1946 State Street. For information call 868–2561.

Three free museums vie for your attention: the **Meeteetse Museum** at 952 Mondell Street, with a collection of historical artifacts and town displays; the **Meeteetse Bank Museum** at 1033 Park Avenue in an old bank building; and the ◆ **Charles J. Belden Museum** at 1947 State Street. It features Charles Belden's world-famous Western and ranch photographs, which have appeared in magazines such as *National Geographic*. The first two museums are open May 15 through September 30 on Monday through Saturday from 10:00 A.M. to 5:00 P.M., and on Sunday from 1:00 to 4:00 P.M. For information call 868–2323. The Belden Museum is open daily May 15 through September 30 from 9:00 A.M. to 5:00 P.M. For information on the museum, call 868–2264.

Charles Belden was co-manager of the famous Pitchfork Ranch founded 18 miles southwest of Meeteetse in 1878. Many of his photographs of the ranch and the West are classics that brought to life the spirit of the western way of life. As Belden used to say, "If the picture doesn't tell a story, it's not worth taking." The Phelps-Belden family still works the ranch.

Meeteetse goes all out for its three-day Labor Day weekend celebrations. Activities include a rodeo, a street dance, an old-time parade, a Western barbecue, 5K and 10K races, and an arts and crafts fair. Meeteetse may no longer have six stage lines running through it or seven bars and eleven brothels, but it still knows how to have a good time. For information call the Meeteetse Tourist Information Center at 868–2603 or write them at Box 509, Meeteetse 82433.

For good grub and a delightful place to stay, try the ◆ **Broken Spoke Cafe and Bed & Breakfast,** next door to the Charles J. Belden Museum in Meeteetse. The building was built in 1894 and renovated one hundred years later in 1994. The cafe features specials and delicious homemade pies every day. Food is plentiful and prices are inexpensive to moderate. The bed and breakfast is located in an upper loft part of the building and is decorated in a Western motif. There are two separate rooms; the larger one includes two bunk beds and a queen-size bed. Room rates are extremely reasonable at $25 per room plus $5.00 for each extra person. A hearty, all-you-can-eat breakfast costs an additional $5.00. For information or reservations call 868–2362.

On the outskirts of Meeteetse, the **Amelia Earhart Monument** marks the famous aviator's love for the area. Earhart was in the process of having a log cabin built in 1937 on the nearby upper Wood River shortly before she disappeared over the Pacific Ocean. The partially completed walls can still be seen near the site of the abandoned Double D Dude Ranch, started in the 1930s. It is located about 2 miles beyond the Brown Mountain Campground, 25 miles southwest of town on the Wood River Road/4DT Road. Beyond the campground, a four-wheel-drive vehicle or travel on foot is required. Inquire about road conditions and specific directions at the U.S. Forest Service offices at 1002 Park Avenue, or call 868–2461.

There are numerous trailheads and campgrounds for hiking or horseback riding adventures. Again, check with the Forest Service for maps of the area.

It's a shame to have to leave Meeteetse, but you'll feel a little better after you arrive in Cody (population 7,897). From Meeteetse take Highway 120 north 31 miles to Cody. Nineteen miles out of Meeteetse pull over to the **Halfway House Stage Stop.** Located halfway between Corbett Crossing and Stinking Water Creek, the stage stop was in use as late as 1908 before automobiles made it obsolete.

As the eastern gateway to Yellowstone, Cody has a lot to offer. Without a doubt, it's a several-day stop to get in everything you'll want to see and experience. With that in mind, you can camp out in the evenings at the ⬥ **Cody Guest Houses.** There are a variety of accommodations to choose from, including the charming Calamity Jane, Buffalo Bill, or Annie Oakley carriage houses; a luxurious three-bedroom Victorian home; a four-bedroom Western lodge; or an executive suite.

The Victorian home's original 1906 front door with leaded stained glass opens into a bygone era. A three-year restoration has made this home a showpiece. Artistic hand stenciling graces walls framed by restored woodwork. You might want to inquire about the work of local artists featured in the gallery. Off the bedrooms upstairs, you can relax in a delightful morning nook. For complete pampering, a gourmet dinner may be requested at an additional fee. Amenities include a spa, hot tub, patio and barbecue, fireplace, and laundry facilities.

Next door, in the Western lodge, you'll experience a different era. Notice the period style of the abundant windows surrounding the living room. Western-related works by local artists and craftspeople abound throughout this spacious home, which can accommodate eight people. After days on the road, you and the kids will enjoy their separate quarters in the lower level. The entertainment center will keep the kids busy.

Each of the guest houses has a kitchen. All units rent by the day or week. The houses can also be rented as a single unit for complete privacy. Peak season rates (June 1 through September 30) run from $85 to $125 per night ($535 to $787 weekly) for the cottages or executive suite to $250 per night ($1,575 weekly) for the Western lodge or Victorian house. Off-season rates are substantially less expensive. The Cody Guest Houses office is located at 1401 Rumsey Avenue. For information or reservations call 587–6000 or (800) 587–6560.

Start your exploration of Cody at **The Irma,** the historic hotel built by Buffalo Bill Cody in 1902 from native wood and limestone. Cody named the hotel after his youngest daughter. Enjoy your lunch or dinner with the ornate cherry-wood bar as a backdrop. The bar was originally valued at $100,00, even more impressive when you consider that the construction cost of the hotel was only $80,000. Buffalo Bill was given the bar by Queen Victoria of England. It was crafted in France and made the journey by freighter to the United States, by rail to Red Lodge, Montana, and by wagon to Cody. The Irma is listed on the National Register of Historic Places. It still operates as a hotel, with renovated rooms furnished in turn-of-the-century motif. Each room is named after a famous person from Cody's colorful history. The Irma is located at 1192 Sheridan Avenue. For information call 587–4221 or (800) 745–IRMA.

Another tie to Buffalo Bill is the world-class ❖ **Buffalo Bill Historical Center,** at 720 Sheridan Avenue. The original museum opened in 1927 in the log structure that now houses the Cody Chamber of Commerce. In actuality, the Historical Center comprises several self-standing museums and galleries in one large facility encompassing 230,000 square feet. Together they tell the story of the West and its peoples, from Native Americans to pioneers. Unlike many museums, the Historical Center displays its exhibits in a spacious environment, inviting the visitor to continue along at a leisurely pace—in order to absorb everything. The sculpture gardens provide a soothing place to contemplate what you have observed.

For the serious historian, there's also the Harold McCracken Research Library's collection of historical photographs, books, and manuscripts, and the Yale Western Americana microfilm collection. The center offers several thirty- to forty-minute interpretative audiotape tours as well as transcripts for hearing-impaired visitors; inquire at the information desk.

In addition, the Historical Center periodically sponsors other major exhibits. For example, in 1995, "Seasons of the Buffalo" showcased the West's most famous animal with a video presentation, photographs, paintings, and interpretive displays, while the "Heart Mountain Relocation Center" photo exhibit illustrated life in the Wyoming Japanese-American relocation camp of World War II.

Annual events hosted at the Buffalo Bill Historical Center include "Cowboy Songs & Range Ballads" with jam sessions and evening concerts in April, the Frontier Festival celebrating frontier skills through competitions and demonstrations in early June, and the Plains Indian Powwow featuring Native American dance competitions in late June. For dates and times call 587–4771 or (800) 227–8483.

The center's original attraction was the Buffalo Bill Museum, established in 1927. It covers the history of the West and the life of William F. "Buffalo Bill" Cody as scout and buffalo hunter and owner of the Wild West Show. You'll discover a rich panorama of Western life, from stagecoaches to Moleworth furniture to a vast selection of Wild West Show memorabilia. Outside, don't miss Buffalo Bill's boyhood home and the larger-than-life sculpture *The Scout*, portraying Buffalo Bill.

The Plains Indian Museum has one of the most extensive and finest collections of Plains Indian art and artifacts. Learn about the various Plains Indian migrations, see how they lived, and experience the beauty and meaning of their art. A particularly interesting exhibit is the collection of Plains Indian moccasins.

The Cody Firearms Museum documents the development of arms from the sixteenth century and houses the world's largest collection of American arms, with more than four thousand firearms.

The Whitney Gallery of Western Art is an impressive and varied collection of work by Western masters. Here you can compare the classic techniques of Frederic Remington and Charles Russell with the contemporary Western art of James Bama and Harry Jackson. You'll be able to study pieces by Albert Bierstadt, George Catlin, and Thomas Moran as well as many other noted artists. Together, they capture the spirit of the West from the nineteenth century to the present day.

A new addition to the Historical Center, The H. Peter and Jeannette Kriendler Gallery of Contemporary Western Art, debuted in 1995. Located in the building's mezzanine, the gallery provides a permanent home for important works by noted contemporary Western painters and sculptors, displaying both traditional and avant-garde art techniques and subjects.

One way to view the Historical Center as a whole is to follow a theme from museum to museum. For instance, the Women in the Galleries brochure available at the information desk examines women in Western art ranging from photographs of Annie Oakley in the Buffalo Bill Museum to Native American women's clothing.

The Buffalo Bill Historical Center is open daily May through October. May and September hours are 8:00 A.M. to 8:00 P.M., June through August hours are 7:00 A.M. to 8:00 P.M., and October hours are 8:00 A.M. to 5:00 P.M. During March, April, and November, the Historical Center is open Tuesday through Sunday with hours of 10:00 A.M. to 3:00 P.M. in March and November and 8:00 A.M. to 5:00 P.M. in April. Admission prices $8.00 per adult with special prices for senior citizens, students, children ages six to twelve, and children ages five and under. For information call 587–4771.

You also won't want to miss the **Cody Mural and Visitor's Center** at Seventeenth Street and Wyoming Avenue. A large mural covers the entire domed ceiling of the chapel foyer of the Church of Jesus Christ of Latter-day Saints and depicts significant historic events during the period 1827–93. Summer tours are given Monday through Saturday 9:00 A.M. to 9:00 P.M. For information call 587–3290.

Old Trail Town puts you right back into the frontier days with the reconstruction of more than twenty historic buildings of the late 1880s. Check out the bullet holes in the door of the Rivers Saloon from Meeteetse, or stop in at the Hole in the Wall Cabin frequented by Butch Cassidy and gang. Old Trail Town brings alive the exciting days of the old West for the whole family. Before you git out of town, visit the cemetery and final resting place for the likes of Jeremiah "Liver-Eat'n" Johnson and buffalo hunter Jim White. Old Trail Town, located at 1831 DeMaris Drive, is open daily from 8:00 A.M. to 8:00 P.M. mid-May through mid-September. For admission rates and information call 587–5302.

Buffalo Bill Cody was an early promoter of building a dam to irrigate the fertile farm land around Cody. The ❖ **Buffalo Bill Dam** was completed in 1910 at a cost of nearly $930,000. The view of the Shoshone Canyon from the glass-walled visitors center or from the open walkway on top of the dam is awesome. The dam is located 6 miles west of Cody on the Yellowstone Highway (Highway 14/16/20). The visitors center is open from approximately May 1 through September 8:00 A.M. to 9:00 P.M. daily. For information call 527–6076.

Along the shore of the reservoir created by the dam lies **Buffalo Bill State Park,** with excellent trout fishing, camping, hiking, and water sports. Entry fees are a few dollars per person and camping is $4.00 per vehicle. For information call 587–9227.

The Shoshone Canyon offers ample opportunity for exciting rafting excursions. **Wyoming River Trips** is Cody's oldest and most experienced river-rafting company, with a number of different rafting trips to choose from. For rates and rafting information call 587–6661 or (800) 586–6661, or write to Box 1541-V, Cody 82414.

Don't leave town without tasting a mouthwatering steak from **Cassie's Supper Club,** a historic Cody landmark that was originally opened in the 1920s and operated as a house of ill repute by owner Cassie Waters. Besides the quality steaks, a variety of chicken, seafood, and pasta dishes await you. Prices are moderate to expensive. After you eat, you can stomp your feet to live country rock music in the saloon on Tuesday through Saturday, join the dance lessons on Wednesday evening, or participate in a Sunday evening jam session where anyone can get up to play or sing. Cassie's is located at 214 Yellowstone Avenue. For reservations or information call 527–5500.

For Italian fare, we recommend **Mamma Mia's** at 1095 Sheridan Avenue. This restaurant offers Italian and American dishes at

Old Trail Town, Cody

moderate prices. Try the Sicilian breaded steak for a change of pace. Open Monday through Sunday for lunch and dinner, 11:00 A.M. to 11:00 P.M. For reservations or information call 587–5711.

Hub Whitt and Candy Hufford of **Great Basin Trail Rides** will custom-prepare any trail ride you desire, for any skill level. As an added bonus, Hub and Candy are talented singers and guitar and fiddle players and will be happy to perform to your heart's content around the campfire. Join in yourself with the old favorites. For information and rates call 868–2477.

President Theodore Roosevelt called the Wapiti Valley between Cody and Yellowstone "the most scenic 50 miles in America." The drive makes a perfect pathway to one of the world's natural wonders. It meanders through Shoshone National Forest, the first national forest in the country, created by President Benjamin Harrison on March 30, 1891. Wapiti Valley offers fast-moving rivers and lazy streams, sheer cliffs and intriguing rock formations, and vast populations of wildlife, from majestic bear and elk to eagles and peregrine falcons.

As beautiful as Wapiti Valley is, we opt for another route into Yellowstone: the newly christened Chief Joseph Scenic Highway, which takes you through equally majestic country with a bit more variation. But first we'll swing up to Powell (population 5,292) before leaving Park County. Take Highway 14A northeast from Cody to Powell. Named after famous explorer Major John Wesley Powell, this town is home to the ◆ **Homesteader's Museum,** which honors the folks who settled in Powell Valley. Located at the corner of Clark and First Streets in a historic log building built in 1932 by Legionnaires, the museum captures the heritage of the area in photographs, artifacts, early tools, and farm machinery that tamed the valley's soils. The museum is open May 1 through September 30 Tuesday through Friday from 1:00 to 5:00 P.M., and the rest of the year on Friday and Saturday from 10:00 A.M. to noon and 1:00 to 5:00 P.M. For information call 754–9481.

On the return to Cody, stop at the **Heart Mountain Relocation Center Monument** located about 12 miles northeast of Cody on Highway 14A. It describes the relocation camp where 11,000 American citizens of Japanese ancestry were confined for nearly three years during World War II. The Heart Mountain Relocation Center was one of ten camps built to house more than 100,000 people. Families were held in detention even if they had family members serving in the U.S. armed forces. This camp was closed in November 1945 and all that remain are a few foundations. A portion of the center is listed on the National Register of Historic Places.

Just before re-entering Cody, take Highway 120 headed northwest and exit to the left onto Highway 289, ◆ **Chief Joseph Scenic Highway,** about 17 miles north of Cody. The road has been widened and turnouts have been constructed for sightseeing and picture-taking, although a few stretches of gravel roadbed remain, scheduled for completion soon. This once-avoided road now serves as a pleasurable trip away from the swarms headed along Yellowstone Highway.

Stop at the top of Dead Indian Pass for a panoramic view that includes the North and South Forks of the Shoshone River, the Beartooth Mountain Range of northern Wyoming and southern Montana, to Yellowstone Park in the west. Sunlight Basin's lush valley to the northwest and majestic snow-peaked mountain ranges and colorful geological upthrusts and bluffs form dramatic vistas.

You are retracing the route Chief Joseph took with his remaining Nez Perce warriors as they fled the U.S. Army in 1877. At Sunlight Creek the highway crosses the highest bridge in Wyoming, 280 feet high. Stop at the side of the road after crossing the bridge and walk back for a great view of the canyon.

The rest of the journey is equally impressive.

WESTERN WYOMING

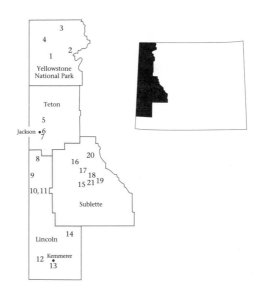

1. Winter in Yellowstone
2. Wolves
3. Petrified Tree
4. Monarch Geyser
5. Chapel of the Transfiguration
6. National Museum of
   Wildlife Art
7. Silver Dollar Bar
8. Grand Canyon of the
   Snake River
9. Cutter and Chariot Racing
10. World's Largest Elk
    Antler Arch
11. Intermittent Spring
12. Fossil Butte National
    Monument
13. J. C. Penney Home
14. Names Hill
15. De Smet Monument
16. Flying A Ranch
17. Box "R" Ranch
18. Fremont Lake
19. Photographer's Point
20. Square Top Mountain
21. Museum of the
    Mountain Man

WESTERN WYOMING

YELLOWSTONE NATIONAL PARK

Staying off the beaten path in Yellowstone National Park is quite a trick since there are only a few designated roads to get you through the park and through the crowds. One tactic is to completely avoid the peak tourist season and postpone your Yellowstone adventure until the winter season. Without a doubt, the park takes on a whole new look with a blanket of snow, even if you have been there dozens of times during the summer.

◆ **Winter in Yellowstone** begins in mid-December and lasts through mid-March. You could also cheat a bit and come in late October or November near the tail end of the regular season, especially if you like fall colors and the crispness of approaching winter. Remember, fall sneaks in a bit sooner and winter arrives with more force in the Yellowstone area than at lower Wyoming elevations. So dress accordingly and bring the proper gear for the coldest weather you anticipate encountering.

During the winter season, Yellowstone is accessible via ten-passenger enclosed and heated snowcoaches, snowmobiles, cross-country skis, and showshoes. That's it—there's no other way to get in, short of parachuting. Warming huts throughout the park provide shelter for a brief rest or for more serious conditions. Overnight accommodations are available at Old Faithful Snow Lodge and Mammoth Hot Springs on the north edge of the park. Room rates range from $42 to $88 per night, and cabins are available at $64 and up. The park offers snowcoach tours, guided ski tours, and snowmobile and cross-country rentals. Skiing lessons are also available. You can drive to Mammoth Hot Springs and begin your winter odyssey from there.

No matter what winter activities you plan to engage in at Yellowstone, you will have an experience you'll never forget. For winter activities, rates, and lodging reservations in Yellowstone, contact TW Recreational Services at 344–7901.

The geysers that are so spectacular in summer are even more fascinating to watch in wintertime. The wildlife also take on a different aspect. Buffalo and elk plowing through the heavy snow are a spectacular sight. Without the hoards of people on the roads clamoring to get photographs, more wildlife can be seen.

And, snowshoes and skis take you on groomed trails where summer visitors are unable to tread. Snow-covered branches and ice glistening around newly erupted geysers, with the Grand Teton Mountains as a backdrop, gives a fairy tale appearance to familiar sights.

For snowmobiles, the newly completed 370-mile Continental Divide Snowmobile Trail from West Yellowstone to the Lander area offers a host of trip possibilities. For a copy of the snowmobile trail map, contact the nearest Bureau of Land Management office. The telephone number for the Cheyenne office is 775–6156 and the Worland district office covering Yellowstone can be reached at 347–9871.

The reintroduction of ♦ **wolves** into Yellowstone resulted in additional thousands of people flocking to the park this past summer. Again, winter is the opportune time to see these controversial creatures without the disturbance of crowds.

The endangered Canadian wolf hadn't been seen in Yellowstone for more than sixty years until their reintroduction during the winter of 1994–95. For the most part, the wolves kept to the Lamar Valley during the summer of 1995 and caused considerable "Wolf Jams" of tourists on the roads. They have since moved out into Pelican Valley and other park locations, probably in search of elk or easier prey. The mature gray wolf (*Canis lupus*) is three times larger than a coyote (*Canis latrans*), typically weighing more than 100 pounds. To determine whether you are sighting a wolf or a coyote, consider the following facts. As mentioned, the wolf's appearance is full-bodied, while the coyote is more slender or delicate in stature. The wolf will reach an average height of 26–34 inches versus only 16–22 inches for the coyote. The above adds up to a weight of 70–120 pounds for a mature wolf and 27–33 pounds for a coyote. The ears of the wolf are rounded and relatively short, and its muzzle is large and broad. In comparison, the coyote's ears are long and pointed and its muzzle is long and narrow. By the way, not all gray wolves are gray; their coats can be almost jet-black or a variety of other shades.

Whether or not you support the reintroduction of wolves in the Yellowstone ecosystem through the current Northern Rocky Mountain Wolf Recovery Plan, the sight of a wolf slinking through the woods or snow meadows, or the sound of a wolf howling at the winter moon, is apt to stir some primeval feelings within your soul. It's *that* haunting an experience. Check with the park about recent wolf sightings and take a pair of binoculars or a zoom lens to get a close-up view of these critters, because they are still in the "avoid humans" mode.

If you *must* travel to Yellowstone during the peak season, the following sights will keep you away from the major crowds and still provide truly unique Yellowstone memories. Coming over from Cody and Park county via Chief Joseph Scenic Highway drops you into the park from one of the least-traveled routes.

The Chief Joseph Scenic Highway was officially dedicated on September 12, 1995, celebrating the completion of a twenty-seven-year, multiproject effort to build and improve one of the most spectacular alpine highways in the West. Incidentally, the finishing of the Chief Joseph closes the last pavement gap in Wyoming's state highway system.

The world's first national park, Yellowstone was created on March 1, 1872, with President Ulysses S. Grant signing the legislation. The park encompasses some 2.2 million acres. Less than 5 percent of the area has been developed. The balance remains wilderness with more than sixty species of mammals, two hundred species of birds, and a half-dozen species of game fish. In addition, the park has twelve tree species and more than eighty types of wildflowers. The lowest elevation is 5,314 feet at the north entrance, and the highest spot is Eagle Peak Summit at 11,358 feet. Entrance fees are $10 per car for a seven-day pass or $15 for an annual pass that also admits you to Grand Teton National Park. The park's regular season is from early May through the beginning of November. For information call 344–7381.

Instead of turning south at the Roosevelt Lodge Junction continue west to an often-missed site, the ◆ **Petrified Tree.** It is located approximately 1 mile west of Roosevelt Lodge. Turn left and follow the signs. The once subtropical tree was buried with volcanic ash and preserved over the ages. Other petrified trees are located at Specimen Ridge.

The **Museum of the National Park Ranger** at Norris is particularly interesting and traces the history of the park ranger profession from soldiers to today's specialists. It gives you a greater appreciation for their work and accomplishments. For information call 344–7353. Another intriguing stop is the **Fishing Bridge Visitor Center** on the north end of Yellowstone Lake.

Petrified tree, Yellowstone

The exhibits on Yellowstone's birds and mammals will help you identify the wildlife you will see during your stay. The center also covers lake geology within Yellowstone. A National Historic Landmark, the center was built in 1929–30. For information call 242–2450.

Stop at the U.S. Engineer's Office in Yellowstone to look at a unique piece of architecture. Designed by the Minneapolis firm of Reed and Stem in 1906, the building is known affectionately as The Pagoda owing to its Oriental appearance. The Engineer's Office is located in Mammoth Hot Springs.

One way to avoid the crowds during the summer months is to take off on the more than 1,200 miles of **hiking trails** within Yellowstone. Travel off the beaten path to the park's thermal features, gorges, rivers, and wildlife sites. Pick up a guide to Yellowstone's hiking trails at the park visitor centers or the Hamilton Stores located throughout the park. Check out the gnarled lodgepole pine used in the porch construction and sign above the entrance of the original **Hamilton Store** near the Old Faithful Inn.

All overnight hikes and some day hikes into restricted areas require backcountry use permits. Apply at the park ranger station or visitors center up to forty-eight hours before beginning your hike. Know your hiking capabilities. As a general rule, plan on one hour for every 2 miles and add an hour for every 1,000 feet you ascend. Check out the topography in advance so you know the difficulty of your proposed hike. Be prepared: Carry a trail map, compass, matches, insect repellent, first-aid kit, knife, and rain gear as a minimum.

For a different look at the park's falls, try the Tower Falls Trail, which comes out at the base. Uncle Tom's Trail is a very strenuous walk that drops about 500 feet in a series of three hundred stairs and paved inclines to the base of the Lower Falls. The North Rim Trail offers several views along its route, including the Artist Point Road Bridge, Crystal Falls, and Upper and Lower Falls. All of these are listed in the pamphlet entitled "Canyon" sold for 25 cents at park visitors centers.

To get even farther away from the crowds, you can expand your hiking ventures into the Greater Yellowstone Area—to the nearby Absaroka/Beartooth Wilderness, one of the highest alpine areas in the nation, or the Shoshone National Forest east of the park.

Yellowstone's volcanic past is evidenced by its geysers and hot springs. Since molten rock is only 3 miles beneath the surface at Yellowstone, the park has the largest and most varied concentration of hydrothermal features in the world. Overall, there are some ten thousand known thermal features here, including nearly two hundred geysers. The geyser is a type of hot spring where pressure builds up underneath the surface of the earth until it finally violently explodes. Some geyers erupt almost continually, while others may lay dormant for months or years. The world's largest geyser, **Steamboat Geyser,** shoots water and steam more than 300 feet in the air, and its eruptions can last up to twelve hours. Steamboat Geyser is located in the Norris Geyser Basin in the Back Basin segment.

As proof that nature is up to her old tricks, the 1964 earthquake reactivated the ◆**Monarch Geyser** for the first time since 1913. It also is located in the Norris Geyser Basin. The **Morning Glory Pool** received its name in 1880 due to its resemblance to the flower. It's a good 2-mile hike from the parking lot near Old Faithful to Morning Glory, so not as many people make the journey to see this beauty. It's located in the Upper Geyser Basin.

Finally, if you want an up-close view of the effects of the 1988 fires, walk the 1-mile **Duck Lake Trail,** which begins near the large mudpot in the parking lot of the West Thumb Geyser Basin.

Wyoming locals in the know avoid the Yellowstone Inn and Lodge and stay at the **Lake Yellowstone Hotel** with its grand pillared entryway and rocking-chair view of Yellowstone Lake. It's listed on the National Register of Historic Places. Rooms are about $80 for annex units and $110 and up per night in the main hotel. For information and reservations call 344–7311 or 242–3708.

TETON COUNTY

Heading south out of Yellowstone you enter the **Grand Teton National Park,** established in 1929 and encompassing almost 500 square miles. One of the youngest mountain ranges on the North American continent, the Tetons are impressive with their dramatic vertical rise and their jagged, snow-covered peaks. The Tetons rise to over 13,000 feet, towering 7,000 feet over the valley meadows below.

Like Yellowstone, Grand Teton offers plenty of hiking opportunities, with more than 250 miles of trails. Several excellent trails start at picturesque glacial Jenny Lake with the Cathedral Group providing an awesome backdrop. For trail conditions and backcountry permits call 739–3300.

Be sure to stop at the ◆**Chapel of the Transfiguration** near Moose. The log chapel was constructed in 1925 and is still in use today. The plate-glass window behind the altar frames the inspiring view of Grand Teton, the tallest peak in the park at 13,770 feet. The park offers a number of **ranger-led activities** such as a fire-and-ice cruise with a discussion of how forest fires and glaciers have shaped the landscape; Native American art and culture discussions; and wildflower hikes and programs for young naturalists.

Inquire at the visitors centers for dates and times of programs. Don't miss the **Indian Art Museum** at the Colter Bay Visitors Center with its fine collection of Native American clothing and art. Collection exhibits include an 1850s Crow shield, smoking pipes, a moccasin case, and basketry. The visitors centers are typically open from mid-May through Labor Day. The Grand Teton National Park can be contacted at 733–2880.

If you are looking for a really unique Western experience in the Tetons or surrounding area, there are several operations that provide either **wagon train rides or dog sled tours.** For wagon train rides contact Wagons West Peterson-Madsen-Taylor Outfitters in Afton at 886–9693 or (800) 447–4711 or Bar-T-Five Teton Prairie Schooner Holiday at 733–5386 or (800) 772–5386. If mushing is your priority call Geyser Creek Dog Sled Adventures in Dubois at 455–2702 or (800) 531–MUSH, Jackson Hole Iditarod Sled Dog Tours at 733–7388, or Washakie Outfitting Outdoor Adventures in Dubois at 733–3602.

The **Gros Ventre River Ranch** (pronounced "grow vahnt"), on the eastern edge of the Grand Teton National Forest along the Gros Ventre River, offers luxurious accommodations in the shadow of the Tetons. The ranch can house thirty-four guests in its electrically heated log cabins and additional guests in the log lodge and homestead house. A short ride or hike takes you to the giant 1925 Gros Ventre Slide, which swept down Sheep Mountain and across the Gros Ventre River and created a lake. The lake burst through its dam in 1927 and demolished ranches downstream as well as the town of Kelly (since rebuilt). Quite a sight.

The Gros Ventre Ranch takes guests by the week or for a three-day minimum. Rates vary by season and type of accommodations. Summer season runs from May 1 through October 31. Winter season runs from December through January 8 for housekeeping cabins only and January 9 through March 31 for accommodations, meals, and use of ranch facilities. For information call 733–4138 or write P.O. Box 151, Moose 83012.

Before you arrive at Jackson there are two worthwhile sights. The **National Elk Refuge** is at the north edge of Jackson. Be on the lookout for elk since thousands of them migrate here for the winter and linger until spring, when they gradually disperse back to their mountain territory. The Jackson Boy Scouts gather the shed antlers and sell them at an auction in the Jackson Town Square, raising thousands of dollars.

On a hill overlooking the refuge sits the 51,000-square-foot ◆ **National Museum of Wildlife Art,** opened in 1994. Its architecture of native materials mirror the surrounding countryside, making the building appear almost like a phantom. The museum's collection consists of more than eighteen hundred pieces of art in a variety of media, from painting to sculpture. More than one hundred artists are featured, including John Audubon, Antoine-Louise Barye, Albert Bierstadt, Carl Runguis, Charles Russell, and Sherry Sander. Its exhibits span more than two hundred years of wildlife art and there's a wonderful outdoor sculpture garden. The facilities include a cafe, an auditorium, and meeting rooms. The National Museum of Wildlife Art is located off Highway 26/89/191 about 3 miles north of Jackson on Rungius Road. For information call 733–5771.

Stop in at the historic Wort Hotel at the corner of Glenwood and Broadway for a glance at the ◆ **Silver Dollar Bar,** inlaid with 2,032 silver dollars. Also check out the display of famous cattle brands in the lobby near the fireplace. JJ'S Silverdollar Bar and Grill serves the best prime rib in town as well as other delicacies. Prices are moderate to expensive. For information call 733–2190.

At the **Sweetwater Restaurant** (733–3553) at the corner of King and Pearl Streets, you can eat indoors or out on the deck. The lamb and trout are crowd pleasers. Prices are moderate to expensive. For Asian fare the **Lame Duck** at 680 East Broadway is a good bet, and **Jedediah's Original House of Sourdough** (733–5671) at 135 East Broadway has great pancakes and other sourdough specialties. For exotic food such as wild game, venture over to the **Blue Lion** (733–3912) at 160 North Millward. Compared to the rest of Wyoming, Jackson restaurant prices run moderate to expensive.

Behind the Wort Hotel at the corner of Glenwood and Deloney is the **Teton County Historical Center,** with an extensive collection of early Jackson-area photographs, Native American bead displays, fur trade artifacts, and an interesting exhibit of pole furniture from the Moosehead Ranch. The museum is open year-round Monday through Friday from 9:00 A.M. to 5:00 P.M. There is a small entrance fee. For information call 733–2414.

Abandoned cabin in the Tetons

Jackson hosts two exceptional events during the year. The **Grand Teton Music Festival** takes place from late June or early July through mid- or late August. Musicians from the leading orchestras, symphonies, and conservatories across the nation journey to Jackson to perform in more than thirty orchestral and chamber music concerts during the summer. For a schedule of performance dates and information, call 733–1128 or write Box 490, Teton Village 83025.

Later in the year, the **Fall Arts Festival** showcases the area's cultural attractions and talents with a variety of exhibits, workshops, and demonstrations. The festival continues for three weeks, while Jackson galleries exhibit the works of regionally and nationally acclaimed artists. Special events include quilting demonstrations, Western art symposium, dance festival, and miniature art show and sale. For dates and activities contact the Jackson Hole Chamber of Commerce at 733–3316 or (800) 443–6931.

One final Jackson sight should be seen: the elk horn entrance-way to the town square, especially beautiful when adorned with Christmas lights during the holiday season.

In keeping with Wyoming's reputation as the Equality State, in 1920 Jackson became the first town in the United States to be governed entirely by women, when town voters elected Grace Miller as mayor and chose women for the four council positions as well city clerk, treasurer, and town marshall. The women remained in office until 1923.

LINCOLN COUNTY

Star Valley and Little Switzerland are nicknames for the isolated but fertile valley region of Lincoln County, southwest of Hoback Junction. You enter the valley via Highway 26/89, traveling along the majestic 3,000-foot-deep ◆ **Grand Canyon of the Snake River.** While the Snake River's white waters head into Idaho, we'll make our first stop at Alpine Junction (population 200), the first of several quaint Mormon villages we'll visit.

Native Americans long valued the moderate climate and lush valley for grazing their horses and hunting for the abundant wildlife. Later, emigrants using the Lander Trail from 1840 to 1870 stopped in Star Valley before continuing on to Oregon. Butch Cassidy and his gang liked the valley's isolation and wintered here away from the pursuit of the law. Mormon leader Brigham Young realized the potential of the rich farmlands and established the first settlement. The area is known for its dairy products, notably cheese, and large, red brick Latter-day Saints churches.

Alpine is a haven for water sports enthusiasts because of its prox-imity to the Grand Canyon of the Snake River and Idaho's Pal-isades Reservoir, as well as being situated at the confluence of the Snake, Greys, and Salt Rivers. With an abundance of hotels and lodges, Alpine makes a great place to headquarter as you explore the nearby river and mountain recreational areas. In mid-June the community hosts the **Good Ole Mountain Days** festival with a country-music jamboree, skill games and contests, a Native Ameri-can jewelry show, a black powder shoot, a tomahawk throw, and a mustache contest. For information call 654–7585.

135

Moving south on Highway 89 takes you through the farming communities of Etna and Freedom. The latter is the headquarters of **Freedom Arms,** a gun manufacturer, and straddles the Wyoming/Idaho border. Freedom is the oldest settlement in the valley, having been established by the Mormons in 1879. The Freedom gun factory makes collector handguns that command a good price.

Stock up on cheese in Thayne (population 267) at the **Star Valley Cheese Factory.** The majority of cheese production is shipped outside the region, some 60,000 pounds annually. You can also grab a bite to eat at the Star Valley Cheese Factory Restaurant. Good sandwiches and great pies. For information call 883–2510.

While Alpine caters to the summer water recreation crowd, Thayne turns to winter and snow to attract visitors, with ◆**Cutter and Chariot Racing.** The All American Cutter Racing Association was organized in Thayne in 1948, but the tradition goes back to the 1920s, when local ranchers and farmers used horse-drawn sleighs to deliver milk to the creamery, pick up supplies, and visit far-flung neighbors.

Taking a page from *Ben Hur,* the chariot races have added wheels to the sleighs. The world's first cutter race took place on Thayne's iced-over main drag. Reportedly, a Latter-day Saints bishop bested a local rancher in the 1920s competition. Interest in the sport has increased over the years since the first World Cutter and Chariot Racing Championship took place in 1965. The horse-pulled chariots race a quarter mile on a straight, snow-covered track. The world record for a quarter-mile cutter race was set in 1994 at 21.64 seconds. Cutter and chariot racing is held in Thayne from the first weekend in December through February. For information call 877–3984.

The **Auburn Rock Church** is one of the oldest buildings in Star Valley and played an important part in local Mormon history. It was constructed of striking rough-cut masonry in the late nineteenth century. Like most Latter-day Saints churches, in addition to serving a religious purpose, it also operated as a community meeting place.

With a population of 1,394, Afton represents the hub of Star Valley. Brigham Young disciple Moses Thatcher founded the town in 1885. Proclaimed the ◆ **World's Largest Elk Antler Arch,** Afton's arch extends over Main Street at a height of 18 feet. It contains more than three thousand antlers. In contrast, the towering steeple of the original Latter-day Saints "Church of the Valley" gives the town a distinct New England feel. An early Scottish resident named the community after Robert Burns's poem, "Flow Gently, Sweet Afton." On a more raucous note, Butch Cassidy reportedly papered the local bar with bank notes from one of his gang's many robberies.

A small museum with a big name, the **Lincoln County Daughters of the Utah Pioneers Museum,** houses a number of pioneer homesteading items, such as a loom and spinning wheel. The museum is located at 46 East Fifth Street. It is open June through August, Monday through Friday from 1:00 to 5:00 P.M., or by appointment. Call 886–3667 for information.

Also erected by the Daughters of the Utah Pioneers is the **Star Valley Marker** at 347 Jefferson Street. The marker commemorates the settling of Star Valley in 1879. An interesting part of the monument is the bell, which originally was housed in an 1892 bell tower and rung every Sunday morning at 9:30 and 9:50 so that valley residents could set their clocks.

Afton is home to Aviat Inc., a company that manufactures some of the finest aerobatic planes. In late June, Afton hosts **Aviation Days** with a demonstration of the Aviat Pitts "Red Baron" aerobatic plane, a hot-air balloon rally, model airplane competitions, and Ultra Lite aircraft demonstrations. For dates and information call 886–3156.

Five miles east of Afton you'll find geologically interesting ◆ **Intermittent Spring.** The natural oddity gushes water for approximately eighteen minutes and then ceases to flow for about the same amount of time. It's one of only a handful of intermittent springs in the world and the only one in the United States. It is believed to expel the highest volume of water. Like Old Faithful, its cycles are fairly predictable. Intermittent Spring functions for nine months of the year. The best time to view it is during high water runoff, from the middle of May through the middle of August. Take Second Avenue East to the dirt road leading to Swift Creek Canyon. You will need to walk a ¾-mile trail to reach the stream from the parking area. It's a pleasant hike with beautiful river and canyon scenery.

For $20 per night you can stay at one of the **Kelly and LaBarge Cabins** in the Bridger-Teton National Forest. Both are old forest ranger stations used when the forest had few serviceable roads and the rangers got around on horseback. The Kemmerer Ranger District Office handles reservations for the rustic cabins, which both require a hike of about 12 miles. The Kelly cabin can be reached from Cokeville by driving 12 miles north on Highway 232 to a trailhead. The trail follows Coal Creek to the northeast before joining up with other trails and turning south to the cabin. The LaBarge cabin can be reached from Afton by driving south on Highway 89 for 14 miles to a trailhead at Fish Creek and then following the trail north easterly to the Smith Fork and the headwaters of LaBarge Creek before turning downhill (south) to the cabin. Cabin facilities include five bunk beds, a wood/gas cookstove, a woodstove for heat, a propane refrigerator, propane lights, and an outhouse. Reservations are required at both cabin locations. For reservations and maps contact the ranger office at 877–4415 or write P.O. Box 31, Kemmerer 83101.

Cokeville was established in 1874 and is the oldest town in Lincoln County. Previously, the town was known as Smith's Fork on the Bear River. The Oregon Trail runs right through town and on into Idaho. Many cutoffs converged near Cokeville, considered the hub of the Oregon Trail, at the ferry site on Smith's Fork. There's an **Oregon Trail Monument** in Cokeville City Park at the corner of East Main Street and Park Street. Keeping up Wyoming's tradition as the Equality State, Cokeville elected a woman mayor and two women council members in 1922.

Follow Highway 30/89 south 19 miles of Cokeville and then proceed on Highway 30 east 14 miles until you reach the entrance to ❖ **Fossil Butte National Monument,** 10 miles west of Kemmerer. The road will take you 3½ miles north to the site. Fossil Butte rises 1,000 feet above Twin Creek Valley to an elevation of 7,500 feet. As its name implies, the 8,180 acres of rugged topography yield the richest freshwater fossil fish deposits in the Western Hemisphere, located in limestone layers from 30 to 300 feet below the surface of the butte. The base of Fossil Butte consists of brightly colored beds of the Wasatch geological formation. The fossil deposits, laid down fifty million years ago, were investigated as early as 1877. The lake-bed fish fossils were later thrust upward to become Fossil Butte. Specimens from Fossil Butte are showcased in museums all over the world.

The visitors center gives you a good orientation and the geologic story of Fossil Butte. You can also obtain hiking maps of the area. Informative trail signs explain the exposed specimens.There are no camping facilites at Fossil Butte, but you can picnic in a small aspen grove about 4 miles from the visitors center. Fossil Butte is open daily from 8:00 A.M. to 4:30 P.M. but closes during winter holidays. For information contact 877–4455.

If looking at fossils isn't exciting enough, you can dig for your own fossils at **Ulrich's Fossil Quarries.** Advance reservations must be made. Excavations take place from June through Labor Day seven days a week from 8:00 A.M. to 9:00 P.M., weather permitting. You will be accompanied by an experienced staff member. Ulrich's furnishes all tools and equipment needed for excavating. Bring your own snacks and liquid refreshments. The quarrying work takes place from 9:00 A.M. to about noon. The $55 fee allows you to collect all specimens except those designated by the State of Wyoming as "rare and unusual." Winter hours for the gallery are 8:00 A.M. to 5:00 P.M. or by appointment. Ulrich's is located off the Fossil Butte road. For reservations or information call 877–6466.

Another type of fossil fueled the growth of Kemmerer (population 3,020), in the form of King Coal. Mahlon S. Kemmerer, for whom the town was named, and his partner Patrick J. Quealy (as in Quealy Dome) opened the area's first coal mine in 1897, establishing the Kemmerer Coal Company. Other ventures proved less successful, as the numerous early mining ghost towns in the hills around Kemmerer attest. Nevertheless, the world's largest coal strip mine is operated here. Mine tours are available; call 877–9081.

Kemmerer's other claim to fame is the opening of the J. C. Penney "Mother Store" under the name of Golden Rule Store by James Cash Penney in 1902. By 1912 there were thirty-four stores and Penney changed the name to J. C. Penney. The Kemmerer store still operates but at a new location. The restored ❖**J. C. Penney Home** makes for an interesting visit. It is located on J. C. Penney Drive across from the Triangle Park. It is open daily during the summer and in the winter by appointment. Inquire at the chamber of commerce or call 877–9761.

The **Fossil Country Frontier Museum** exhibits the region's cultural and historical past. A unique summer program involves local citizens presenting Campfire Chats about the area's colorful history. The museum is located at 400 Pine Street and is open daily from 9:00 A.M. to 5:00 P.M. For information call 877–6551.

Lincoln County Courthouse (circa 1925) has been restored and is worth a tour to see the fine dome and art deco and Native American features. The adjoining jail has been recycled to house a fine collection of fossils. The courthouse and jail are located on Sage Avenue. On the other side of the law, a woman named Madame Isabelle operated a "house of ill fame" that garnered enough money for her to build a gracious house at 301 Ruby Street.

Kemmerer's sister city Diamondville is home to delicious Italian cooking at **Luigi's Supper Club** at 819 Susie Avenue. Prices are moderate and the choices are mouthwatering. For information call 877–6221.

Tragedy along the Oregon Trail and other trails headed westward is etched into the Wyoming landscape. Historians estimate that from one in ten to one in seventeen of the 350,000 emigrants who traveled the Oregon Trail died along the way, an average of ten deaths for each mile of the route. The major danger was cholera, followed by accidents involving livestock, wagons, firearms, and river crossings. Contrary to popular myth, Indians were a minor danger in terms of the numbers of deaths.

Seventeen miles northwest of Kemmerer on Highway 233 are the graves of two who met their fate along the trail. Nancy Jane Hill was traveling in 1852 with a wagon train that was delayed for more than two weeks by Indian attacks. Although she survived the Indian threat, she succumbed to cholera and died on July 5 at the age of twenty. Her fiancé is said to have returned to her grave site three times over the next fifty-three years.

Alfred Corum and three brothers left Missouri in 1849 to seek their fortunes in the goldfields of California. Their wagon reached Hams Fork Plateau on July 3 and stopped because Alfred had been sick for over a week. As the brothers tended to his needs, more than two hundred wagons passed them on the dusty trail during the day. Alfred died on Independnce Day of unknown causes.

Before you leave Kemmerer, check the weather and road conditions. The road to the grave sites is rough and can be unpassable in wet weather.

Our final Lincoln County stop, ◈**Names Hill,** is the third of the three Oregon Trail registers where emigrants carved their names into eternity. Like Register Cliff near Guernsey and Independence Rock southwest of Casper, Names Hill evokes a haunting presence along the Oregon Trail. It is located several miles south of LaBarge off Highway 189. Nearby Fontenelle Reservoir offers camping and picnicking facilities.

SUBLETTE COUNTY

Trappers and hunters used the Green River Valley for a number of their rendezvous, coming here to obtain supplies for the coming season and sell or trade the results of their current efforts. Altogether there were sixteen Rocky Mountain rendezvous, six of which were held in the "Valley of the Green" area. The first rendezvous occurred in 1825 within 20 miles of the confluence of Henry's Creek and the Green River, south of present-day Granger in Sweetwater County. The event lasted only one day as trappers traded beaver and other pelts for needed supplies. Later gatherings carried on for more than a week and attracted all sorts of characters who participated in the revelry of horse racing, skill contests, wrestling bouts, gambling, and yarn spinning. By the 1830s, dwindling fur supplies and changes in fashion were signaling the end of the once-bustling fur trade. The final rendezvous took place in 1840 along the Seedskeedee (Green River) near present-day Daniel in Sublette County. This was also the site for the 1833, 1835, 1836, 1837, and 1839 rendezvous.

Drive northwest out of LaBarge on Highway 189 to Big Piney (population 454) and stop at the **Green River Valley Museum** for an introduction to the valley's history. The museum has an interesting brand exhibit dating back to 1895 and the original oil Wardell Buffalo Trap Mural featured on the 1995 Wyoming Archaeological Society poster. The museum is located on Highway 189 in Big Piney. It is open Tuesday through Saturday from noon to 4:00 P.M.

Just before you arrive at Daniel, there's a historical marker about Father De Smet on the right side of Highway 189. The marker commemorates the one hundredth anniversary of the first Roman Catholic mass said in Wyoming, which occurred on July 5, 1840. To find the actual ❖ **De Smet Monument** and spot where Father De Smet said mass, follow the gravel road marked Daniel Cemetery for about 3 miles. You get a wonderful view of the valley and Green River from this vantage point. There's also a granite monument here and a small chapel built of native rock.

141

Nearby is the grave site of Pinckey Sublette, one of the brothers of William Sublette, the famous fur trader and discoverer of the Sublette Cutoff for whom Sublette County was named. Pinckey's body made a few journeys after his death in 1865. He was exhumed in 1897 and shipped off to St. Louis, where he remained until 1935 when a court order returned him to Sublette County.

If you are looking for a week or more of great fly fishing, horse-back trail rides into the mountains, fantastic vistas in the shadow of the Gros Ventre Range, and gourmet meals then let ranch manager Debbie Hansen and her staff at the ◆ **Flying A Ranch** pamper you. Built in 1929, the historic ranch has been completely refurbished while retaining its original character. You'll find yourself enjoying total comfort in a grand Western atmosphere. Six spacious handcrafted homestead log cabins each provide a large sitting area, kitchenette, and private bath. Most have a fireplace or woodburning stove for additional ambience. Appropriately, each cabin is named after an early settler in the valley.

For dinner the Flying A features a combination of Western fare and continental cuisine, but before you feast on the shrimp scampi, Italian delicacies, or Mexican fare, cocktails are served at the pondside Gilded Moose Saloon facing the mountains. The ranch caters to couples, not families, so revel in your escape time away from your kids and those of others. Rates run around $1,000 per week per person based on double occupancy with a discounted schedule after September 1. The Flying A Ranch season runs from mid-June to late-September. For information during the season call 367–2385 or write to them at Route 1, Box 7, Pinedale 82941. During the off-season call (605) 332–0946 or (800) 678–6543 or write 301 North Dakota Avenue, Sioux Falls, South Dakota 57102. Call early because the ranch books up fast with return guests and discriminating newcomers. The Flying A Ranch is located 27 miles northwest of Pinedale and 16 miles southeast of Bondurant off Highway 191. Watch for the ranch sign on the right side of the road as you head northwest. The gate to the entrance gate is locked, so call ahead for directions and the lock combination.

For a real working cattle ranch experience try the ◆ **Box "R" Ranch** near Cora. The ranch has been in the Lozier family for four generations, first homesteaded in 1898 and moving in on its "centennial ranch" designation. Once you've reached this secluded getaway, you'll notice the Loziers' pride and joy right away, the very large horse barn with a roofed saddling area.

The scenery is fantastic—it's the only deeded land on the border of the Bridger Wilderness Area. Your very own mount for trail rides during the length of your stay will be chosen from seventy-five horses and mules. Plus you'll get to help round up cattle (early, early in the morning) and move them to new grazing ground. Hearty meals are served ranch-style with the wranglers and guests eating together. If you've got the gumption and are handy with a tool or two, you can dig in and help Irv Lozier and his son Levi mend fences or erect a new guest cabin.

The Loziers offer seven ranch and mountain vacations to fit your needs, ranging from a week of cattle drives to full-service wilderness pack trips. The Loziers are proud of their ranching heritage and run a very efficient outfit. Irv is quite well-versed on the ranching and geologic history of the area, and you can get him to bend your ear a bit with a little prodding. Be sure to ask him about glacial activity in the land surrounding the ranch.

Prices start around $795 weekly per person, double occupancy. The Box "R" Ranch season runs from late May through mid-September. For complete rates and other information call 367–2291. For reservations call (800) 822–8466 or write Box 100, Cora 82925.

Considered the doorway to the Winds (Wind River Mountains), Pinedale is the embarking spot for many different wilderness adventures, from half-day trips to week-long excursions. The Wind River Mountains encompass fifteen of Wyoming's highest peaks, with Gannett Peak, almost directly north of Pinedale, the crowning jewel at 13,804 feet. In the Winds you can also explore 400,000 acres of Bridger-Teton Wilderness, twenty-seven active glaciers, more than 1,300 alpine lakes, and approximately 600 miles of trails from nine different trailheads. For information contact the Pinedale Area Chamber of Commerce at 367–2242 or the Pinedale Ranger District at 367–4326.

Four miles north of town on Fremont Lake Road (154), ◆ **Fremont Lake**'s pristine beauty sits at the base of the Wind River Mountains and captivates your spirit. It is Wyoming's second largest natural lake and one of the deepest and purest lakes in the nation. Famous for its large fish, Fremont Lake once gave up a record-breaking forty-pound mackerel. Spend a day fishing, wading, or swimming at the sandy beach, or camp overnight. Boat rentals and lake tours are also available. The lake was named after explorer John C. Fremont.

Skyline Drive, beginning at the east end of Pine Street, takes you on a 26-mile, hour-long loop drive through a scenic panorama of lakes, mountains, and valleys. Along the loop you'll come to Elkhart Park, where you can detour on a hike to ◆ **Photographer's Point** in the Bridger-Teton Wilderness. The trail is well marked and delivers a fantastic view of Fremont Peak and the Continental Divide across a deep glacial valley. The round trip covers about 8 miles.

A longer loop tour takes you on a 100-mile round-trip jaunt promising postcard-perfect images of wildlife, mountain scenes and alpine lakes. The highlight of the trip, a gigantic monolith known as ◆ **Square Top Mountain,** towers over the headwaters of the Green River at 11,679 feet. The intriguing mountain was carved by a glacier out of the granite core of the Wind River Mountain Range over eons. As an added bonus, you will see the beautiful **Green River Lakes.** Take Highway 191 west 6 miles and then head north on Highway 352. After the road turns to gravel, travel another 20 miles to reach Green River Lakes and Square Top Mountain. Along the way you'll pass Kendall Warm Springs, home to the Kendall dace, a two-inch-long fish. The remains of Wyoming's first dude ranch, Billy Wells Ranch, are also along this stretch of road. Be alert for moose, elk, and deer. The Green River Lakes parking area marks the jumping-off spot for day hikes and longer trips. You can camp overnight at the Green River Lakes Campground or nearby Whiskey Grove.

A number of Pinedale area outfitters can take you on a wide variety of adventures in the Winds. **Wind River Hiking Consultants** at 367–2560 provides topographic maps, trail information, accommodations and transportation for backpacking trips. **Wind River Resort Outfitters** at 367–2109 in Daniel runs full-service summer and fall day rides, fully guided pack trips, and gear drops for the more adventuresome and experienced. In addition to the above, **Bridger Wilderness Outfitters** at 367–2268 adds some different options, such as summer and winter wilderness survival courses; youth camps teaching first aid, horseback riding, and leadership skills; fly-fishing packing trips;

hunting camps; and the DC Bar Guest Ranch, one of the oldest guest ranches in the area.

In Pinedale, make it a point to spend a few hours in the ◆ **Museum of the Mountain Man.** It's located on the east edge of town just off Highway 191 at the top of the hill as you head north on Fremont Lake Road. You'll be treated to an excellent presentation on the fur trading era and the life of the mountainman. Look for Jim Bridger's rifle. The kids will like the hands-on exhibits, such as the beaver fur that invites you to "Please touch me." Special programs and living-history demonstrations are scheduled during the summer season, and there are additional exhibits on the Plains Indians, tie hacking, and pioneer ranching life. The museum is lively and spacious, a delightful start or end to the day. It leaves a mark on the landscape of your imagination. The museum is open May 1 through October 1 daily from 10:00 A.M. to 6:00 P.M. Call 367–4101 for winter hours or other information. The entrance fee is $4.00 for adults and $2.00 for children.

In early July, Pinedale hosts **Rendezvous Days** with a reenactment of the 1830s rendezvous when trappers, traders, and Native Americans gathered at the Green River. Events include a two-hour award-winning pageant (Wyoming's oldest), rodeos, concerts, historic demonstrations, a discussion of Plains Indian culture, and a pit-roasted buffalo. For information call 367–4101.

The 1929 **Log Cabin Hotel,** a National Historic Landmark, rents nine cabins and two rooms in the main building. Many have cooking facilities and television. At one time, ownership of the motel changed hands in a poker game. For rates and information call 367–4579. The **Window on the Winds B&B** serves up a great breakfast after a soak in the hot tub and a night in your rustic bedroom and lodgepole bed. The bed and breakfast is located at 10151 Highway 191 in Pinedale. For reservations call 367–2600.

McGregor's Pub, at 21 North Franklin Avenue, serves a variety of excellent dishes from prime rib to fresh fish at moderate to expensive prices. For reservations call 367–4443.

It's fitting that we should end our tour of Wyoming at Pinedale, near the site of the last rendezvous more than a century and a half ago. It makes for a striking comparison between long-ago Wyoming and that of today. Although the emigrants and wagon trains, cavalry soldiers and active forts, and fur trade and mountain man are long gone, the pioneer spirit and the raw land of Wyoming live on virtually unchanged through the centuries. We're sure that whether you live in Wyoming or not, in some unexplainable, intangible way, the state and its people have touched your soul. One of our friends remarked after a visit that Wyoming had changed her perspective on life. She calls it "the miracle of Wyoming." Happy trails.

INDEXES

General Index

147

Bed and Breakfasts, Hotels, Inns, and Lodges

Guest Ranches

Box "R" Ranch, 142
Brush Creek Ranch, 27
Diamond Guest Ranch, 56
Flying A Ranch, 142
Gros Ventre River Ranch, 132
High Island Ranch & Cattle
  Company, 110
Lazy L & B Ranch, 76
Terry Bison Ranch, 8
Vee Bar Guest Ranch, 21

Restaurants and Saloons

Atlantic City Mercantile, 72
Bailey's Bar & Grill, 90
Blue Lion, 133
Busy Bee Lunch, 102
Cafe Jacques, 17
Cassie's Supper Club, 121
Cheyenne Cattle Company, 8
Chugwater Soda Fountain, 57
Ciao's, 94
Club El Toro, 69
Coal Creek Coffee Company,
  17
Cowboy Saloon & Dance Hall,
  17
Fabulous Fifties Diner, 17
Farson Mercantile, 39
Goose Egg Inn, 64
Green River Brewery, 42
Grubs, 39
Hong Kong Restaurant, 90
Jedediah's Original House of
  Sourdough, 133
Jeffrey's Bistro, 17
Jeffrey's Two, 17
Lame Duck, 133
Log Inn, 39
Lollypops, 26
Luigi's Supper Club, 140
Magpie, 69
Mamma Mia's, 121
Matilda's, 8
McGregor's Pub, 145
Mi Casa Cafe, 33
Mint, 94
Old Corral, 23
Old Mill Inn, 88
Old Miners' Bar, 53
Old Yellowstone Garage, 79
Overland Restaurant, 16
Paisley Shawl, 61
Pantry Restaurant, 35
Park Grill, 39
Pete's Ruck 'N Rye, 44
Pumpernick's, 108
Rita's Fine Mexican Food, 42
Seney's Drugs, 102
Sheridan Inn, 92
Silver Dollar Bar, 133
Sorells, 46
Spotted Horse, 91
Svilar's Bar & Dining Room,
  68
Sweetwater Grille, 69
Sweetwater Restaurant, 133
Venice Bar, 54
White Mountain Mining
  Company, 39
Yellowstone Drug Store, 67

ABOUT THE AUTHORS

Richard J. Maturi is a full-time freelance writer who is the author of more than one thousand published articles and seven books on investing. His work has appeared in *American History,* the *Akron* (Ohio) *Beacon Journal,* the *Casper* (Wyoming) *Star-Tribune,* the *Denver Post, Equine, Executive Living, Plain Dealer Magazine,* and other regional and national publications.

Mary Buckingham Maturi is an artist, researcher, and co-author with Richard of *Cultural Gems: An Eclectic Look at Unique United States Libraries.* Mary and Richard are working on a book about Francis X. Bushman, an early screen star.

Other books by Richard J. Maturi:

Wall Street Words
Divining the Dow
Stock Picking
Money Making Investments
Main Street Beats Wall Street
The 105 Best Investments for the 21st Century
The Hometown Investor

Also of Interest from The Globe Pequot Press

Guide to Ancient Native American Sites $15.95
Discover the marvels of America's pre-Columbian past.

Discover Historic America: The Wild West $16.95
A family-oriented guide to touring America's Frontier cities and towns

Enduring Harvests $14.95
Native American Foods and Festivals for Every Season

Recommended Country Inns:
   The Rocky Mountain Region, 5/e $14.95
The best inns in the region

Quick Escapes in the Pacific Northwest, 2/e $14.95
40 weekend trips from Portland, Seattle, and Vancouver, B.C.

Other titles in this series:

Off the Beaten Path guides are available for every state in the country and parts of Canada.

Available from your bookstore or directly from the publisher. For a free catalogue or to place an order, call toll-free 24 hours a day (1–800–243–0495), or write to The Globe Pequot Press, P.O. Box 833, Old Saybrook, Connecticut 06475-0833.